The Numbers Business

How to grow a successful cloud accountancy practice

Della Hudson FCA

The Numbers Business
How to grow a successful cloud accountancy practice
ISBN 978-1-912300-16-7
eISBN 978-1-912300-17-4

Published in 2018 by SRA Books
© Della Hudson 2018

Printed in the UK.

Dedication

To those who have always encouraged me to fly high because failure is nothing to be feared when you are loved unconditionally: my parents, Sylvia and Terry Gibson.

To my fabulous team at Hudson Business Accountants and Advisers who have travelled this journey with me.

To the inspirational and supportive friends I have met along the way.

To my children: dream big, surround yourselves with great people and don't be scared to ask for help.

Foreword

In this book, Della Hudson shares the essence of how she succeeded in today's increasingly dynamic world of small business accounting and advisory services. It doesn't stop there: she also provides step-by-step practical hints and tips with incredible detail and clarity.

I know that being described as an early adopter bemuses Della somewhat. But, from my perspective at Xero, she was one of the very first professionals in the UK to recognise and seize the opportunity of cloud software and digital processes in transforming client service. What's more, her firm's internal efficiency and profitability have shone through at every stage of the journey.

Today, the changes unfolding within the accounting industry that prompted Della to act are not just well underway, they are also gathering pace and increasingly challenging and reshaping long-held thinking and principles in the accounting industry. This has no doubt prompted a growing number of professionals to draw up their own plans.

To that end, reading this book is akin to borrowing Della's personal notebook. It shines a light on how she achieved great success amid this period of change, and every single lesson she learned along the way

Gary Turner
Co-founder and managing director at Xero UK

Contents

Introduction

This is the manual that I wanted when I first set up my accountancy business in 2009. I read plenty of generic business books and downloaded some great material from the Institute of Chartered Accountants of England and Wales (ICAEW) website but there were so many gaps that I had to make up for myself as I went along. Had I bought a franchise or an existing accountancy firm, it would hopefully have come with a full instruction book but it would also have come with a high price tag.

This is the story of how I set up my own practice. It is deliberately partisan as it is based on my own experience. So please, take what's helpful to you now. The rest might come in useful later.

This book is a road map that will help a qualified professional to:

- ▶ start a successful business from scratch with no personal or business contacts
- ▶ recruit and train a team of technical and administrative staff
- ▶ move from the kitchen table to external premises
- ▶ create a highly systemised business, which can function independently of the business owner
- ▶ run an ethical business, which contributes to the local community
- ▶ host and speak at business events
- ▶ set up a marketing system that operates even during the busiest periods in order to grow the business organically
- ▶ purchase a business
- ▶ sell a business.

Mine was an accountancy business, but most of this applies to other professional service businesses too. This is one way. It is not the only way but I hope that it helps you to find your way. I'm sure that you can make plenty of your own mistakes, so please feel free to learn from mine.

And to provide a little extra help, there is a list of further resources at the end of the book.

Chapter 1
Understanding your motivation

Finding your why

It is very important to work out why you want to run your own business.

The most common reasons I come across for starting up on your own come under the following headings:

- ▶ To make, and keep, more cash for yourself
- ▶ To have a better work–life balance
- ▶ To have flexibility for family or other commitments
- ▶ To be your own boss

Running a business is hard work and can take over your life. The buck stops with you. There may be months when you are putting money into the business that you thought would be supporting you. When you're working silly hours while you were hoping to work less. Keeping yourself going through these tough times often comes down to knowing, and remembering, why you're doing it.

Take some time to work out what feels good in your present role and what is missing. Now focus on what you expect to feel in your new role as business owner. The things that are positives in both are likely to point towards your motivators. You may find it useful to do this exercise on your own where you can be completely honest with yourself. I would also suggest doing it with somebody who knows you well personally as they may be able to give you some insight into what they think makes you tick.

Good reasons to start your own business:

- ▶ I'm prepared to work hard to get ahead
- ▶ I can see ways to do things better
- ▶ Flexible working that is not available elsewhere
- ▶ I have an idea
- ▶ I've always wanted to run my own business

Poor reasons to start your own business (although these may be good reasons to change your job):

- ▶ It's a quick way to make more money
- ▶ I have a dreadful boss
- ▶ I want an easy life

Capture these motivators somehow. Useful methods are:

- ▶ Dreams and desires folder. If you are looking for affluence this could be pictures of your ideal car or second home.

- ▶ Mood board. If you are aiming for freedom then add pictures of what this represents to you. If you want a better balance then a picture of your family may be one of the things on your board. Include a few meaningful quotes too.

- ▶ Perfect day. Write a description of a typical day in your new life. As well as paying attention to the actual work element, think what you will do with your own time and money and how you hope people will regard you.

- ▶ List. This might seem dull but a simple list of what you want out of your business is the right way for some people to motivate themselves.

- ▶ A phrase that encapsulates your purpose. It needn't be a full explanation of what you want to get out of your business. This is not your business purpose that you may need to share with employees but something simple that reminds you of your reason for doing it.

Once you have established your personal motivation you can move on to planning your business in the next chapters.

My story

I had never had any desire to run my own practice. I'd considered it several times over the years but never felt sufficiently passionate to submit myself to the stress of being my own boss. Although I usually work pretty hard I wasn't sure that I had the self-discipline to do it for myself either (It turns out that I did!). After qualifying as a chartered accountant in a practice in London, I moved to The Midlands and made the change across into management accounting and financial control.

The type of companies I worked for meant that I was usually part of the management team responsible for running the local operation of a multinational business. Thus I was expected to have a broad range of knowledge but could call on experts at head office. In my different roles I have been responsible for: finance, accounting, IT, human resources (HR), premises, quality, environmental sustainability and almost everything else apart from distribution and sales.

This proved to be perfect training for running my own business where I was expected to know everything or to pay an expert where absolutely necessary.

The reason that I eventually set up my own business (and also the reason I sold it) was my family. I wanted:

Interesting, professional work that fits around family life.

This was written in the front of my very first planning notebook and I referred to it several times over the years when difficult or large decisions had to be made.

This placed a big constraint on my activities in that I had to set up and then grow my business on an average of just 25 hours per week. This compares to other business owners who often work 50–60 hours per week, and 80 hours is quite common. Every hour had to be productive. It wasn't about maximising my income but increasing my income per hour. As a consequence I became very good at systemising, delegating and automating. This knowledge and experience meant that I was able to do a lot of work with business owners working silly hours who wanted methods to recover the life part of their work–life balance.

This is why you need to be clear on your own motivation so that you do not sacrifice your *raison d'être* for a good but inappropriate goal.

Imposter syndrome

When running a business it is very easy to focus on what still needs to be done and to forget how much you have achieved. Whenever somebody describes you as inspirational your mind flits to all the things that you haven't done. You might even feel that you are unworthy of their praise, and this is known as the imposter syndrome.

It is quite common amongst successful people and you may need to take action to boost your own confidence:

▶ Document your achievements on a fairly regular basis. This can be privately or as part of meetings with a business coach.

▶ Celebrate your successes. Open a bottle of something fizzy, treat yourself to something or just allow yourself to feel pleased and proud for a moment.

▶ Be proud of your achievements. If you would compliment someone else for it then you should certainly be kind to yourself.

Support team

Running a business is hard work. It is easier if you have a good support team around you. There are various people whom you might want as part of your team:

- A business coach or mentor will help you to see the wood from the trees. Even though you may know what you are doing it is good to have somebody to hold you to account and to make sure that you follow plans through. They will act as a critical friend.
- A critical friend who will be on your side but will challenge your ideas. Even if they don't understand running a business or accountancy they can still be of help.
- A board of directors and non-executive directors will provide you with the same guidance as your coach plus specific expertise in different areas. You will need to check your professional body's rules on management and control.
- A collaboration group, either formal or informal, which can be made up of other accountants from outside your area or other local business owners. You can share best ideas and help each other through your experience. You will achieve more with your time if you do this formally with a facilitator.
- A business partner, especially if their skills complement your own.

Don't forget that, with any of these, you will need to bear in mind client confidentiality as well as your own business confidentiality.

Outside the business environment you may need practical support to enable you to work. This may come from your family and friends or paid help such as childcare and cleaners. Build your support network and make sure that you show your appreciation for them.

Avoiding pitfalls

- Ensure that you have enough cash to live on for at least 12 months. This can come from savings, part-time work or alternative income. This is in addition to the cash that you need for the business and will allow you to take the best decisions for your business, instead of the cheapest ones.
- Listen to advice but remember that your goal is personal to you so examine every piece of wisdom to decide if it will move you closer to your goal.
- Never waste a good idea. Even if it isn't right for now keep a file of ideas so that you can collate them when you have time or need.

Summary

▶ Know why you are in business (your personal/life goal) so that you are able to focus on getting what you want personally.

▶ Know your business goal to help you to achieve your personal goal.

▶ Set up a support network of trusted friends and advisers.

▶ Running your own business is not right for everybody and reading this book should help to give you an idea if this is right for you as well as an idea of how to go about it.

Chapter 2
Establishing your systems
and services

Create systems for all the regular processes within your business. Right from day one. These can start out as checklists and templates, which become proper procedures as you begin to take on staff. The procedures will constantly evolve as your business grows and you discover better ways of doing things. In a growing business your written procedures will need constant review if they are to reflect what is actually happening for more than a few months at a time.

Pros of systemising

Systemising your business will give you some or all of the following benefits. It will:

- make it easy to carry out work to a similar (high) standard each time
- make it easier to train your first employee
- make it easier to delegate to your existing team
- make it easier to automate processes
- make the business less dependent on you so that it is more saleable
- enable you to take a holiday with confidence
- allow you to carry out more work in the same time as you don't need to reinvent the wheel each time, therefore increasing profits.

Cons of systemising

There are no real cons of having a properly systemised business apart from the time it takes to keep documentation up to date.

Jobs that you can systemise

- Accounts production, tax returns, bookkeeping, payroll, and management accounts are the obvious starting points
- Marketing activities
- Event planning, promotion and follow-up
- Answering phones and taking messages
- Handling client enquiries
- Onboarding new clients
- Disengaging unsuitable and other clients
- Following up after networking

- ▶ Chasing client information in before you can commence work
- ▶ Sending client information out for signature and submission
- ▶ Standardised training workshops and so on
- ▶ Template letters and emails

How can you systemise?

1. Read Michael Gerber's (2001) *E-Myth* book for a detailed method
2. Pareto or 80:20 rule. Start with your main processes first
3. Map out the process with wallpaper, or rolls of drawing paper and sticky notes
4. Write this up as the existing procedure, warts and all, so that you have a base that (sort of) works
5. Now repeat the mapping and include any improvements
6. Write up this improved procedure
7. Complete the task yourself by only following the procedure
8. Add whatever extras you need
9. Get somebody else to complete the task by following the procedure
10. Add whatever extras you need
11. Review the process regularly to:
    - ▷ Make sure that it is working
    - ▷ Add any variations that you hadn't originally identified
    - ▷ Improve your processes
12. Quality should be a process of continuous improvement

My story

Back in 2009 I was preparing accounts on Excel and using Her Majesty's Revenue and Customs (HMRC) online software to prepare and submit the tax returns. I started with a checklist just for me to ensure that I hadn't forgotten anything.

As the business grew I could afford to invest in tax and accounts software, which automated the number crunching part of the business. This meant that the procedure needed to be updated.

I took on my first employee and the checklist became a procedure, which I could use for training my new starter. Although he was part way through studying for Association of Accounting Technicians (AAT) qualifications he had never worked in an accountancy company before. The procedure needed more detail.

While I was delegating work as single tasks I was still essential to the business as I was always controlling the workflow. Holidays included one telephone conversation per day back to the office. I realised that I needed standard working papers so I devised something on Excel. For the small jobs the work evolved so that I was just reviewing the accounts, tax and working papers once the work was completed. I was now able to take a step away from the business to look at making improvements.

I realised that a bottleneck was the poor quality of information coming in from clients. To improve this we created a standard bookkeeping spreadsheet for them and showed them how to use it. Training individual clients took up a lot of my time so we started running basic bookkeeping workshops to train up to six people per week on how to use our spreadsheet. This was free to our own clients but we charged non-clients. They sat alongside our own clients who told the non-clients how wonderful we were. They were doing our marketing for us! It was also useful to help the smallest companies who didn't really need an accountant. The quality of information coming in was improving so we didn't need to charge some of the clients for bookkeeping services.

We introduced a second member to the team. This allowed us to handle more work but also meant that there was a second qualified and experienced accountant to handle the gaps where there weren't any procedures. Remember that we've only attacked the biggest processes so far.

This second person meant that my role became about half business development, that is, generating more business *and* improving our existing processes, and half accounts work.

I set up a second process for collecting all the information and generating all the paperwork for new clients. This took about two hours per client. Sometimes prospects would say yes then change their minds and never complete the paperwork, so the initial meeting and this paperwork were a waste of time.

This two hours was quickly reduced to just 30 minutes by using templated engagement letters and online signatures. (We used Signable, a local business, and I would highly recommend them.)

The accounts and tax returns were also signed online. This saved paper and reduced the usual turnaround time from around one week to a matter of minutes. The saving on stationery more than covered the Signable subscription.

I took on a part-time personal assistant (PA). I had used a virtual PA previously but found that in-house suited us better, especially once we had a reception desk to man in our new offices. This meant that I had now delegated the 30-minute routine. So now we had our two repetitive systems documented, partially automated and almost fully delegated.

We had also grown the team and, once again, I was the bottleneck at the review stage. We introduced a process whereby all work was completed or reviewed by a qualified accountant. We ensured general quality through our internal systems and some of our software had basic cross-checks. We also provided internal (monthly lunch and learn) and external training to all team members.

Quality is a continuous improvement process so we might, for example, discuss ways to improve the year-end process for next year's self-assessment 'rush'. Or how to get better information from our clients through providing training on the Xero software or bringing the bookkeeping to us or another qualified bookkeeper. Or how to make our accounts reviews slicker. We also kept improving our workflow software.

By the time I sold the business my role was almost entirely business development and business advice. This was by virtue of my qualifications and my experience running Hudsons and larger businesses prior to that. The next step would have been to find another business adviser who could take on this element of my role by following and improving my systems.

So that's how we automated, delegated and generally systemised our business, and I loved helping clients to improve theirs too.

Who can help?

See 'Further resources' for useful software.

You might use an independent consultant to help map and improve your processes, or as a facilitator in the mapping, a source of new ideas and an extra pair of hands.

Avoiding pitfalls

It could become a full-time role documenting the ever-changing systems in a growing business, but the important thing is to communicate with your team. Not only will they have to follow these procedures but they may also have good ideas on how to improve them.

Summary

▶ Once you've grown your business to a certain size you may want to step up or step out (at least a little bit as the 80 hours or so per week is unsustainable).

▶ Mapping your existing systems is important to maintain consistent standards as you grow.

▶ Your system maps are also the starting point of your continuous improvement process, either by improving the individual system or by systemising more processes.

▶ Documenting processes and training your team are the key to unlocking your own time as you will be able to delegate more.

▶ Don't be afraid to automate these processes where possible.

Chapter 3
Dealing with the formalities

Where to start when setting up your business? Initially, there is likely to be quite a bit that you don't yet know but here are some of the necessary things to consider in the beginning stages.

Should I be a limited company or a sole trader?

It is much simpler to set up as a sole trader and, these days, there are not so many tax advantages of trading through a limited company.

Advantages of a limited company:

- ▶ Limited liability as the company is a separate legal entity from you. It can own property, sue and be sued. In practice a lot of the risk is covered by professional indemnity and other insurances
- ▶ There may be tax advantages, although how much will depend on your personal circumstances
- ▶ Formal structure if you have other principals
- ▶ A limited company gives the impression of being larger than a one-man band

Disadvantages of a limited company:

- ▶ Increased administration

There are, of course, many additional trading formats but, generally, more complexity means more administration time and cost.

Choosing a name

These days choosing a name also involves checking which suitable domain names are free. Your main domain name will be most effective if it is similar to the trading name of your company. It should also be fairly clear what you do. Make it easy for people: I first traded as Hudson & Co and had to keep clarifying that we were accountants and not solicitors.

Your professional body may have restrictions over the type of name you can use.

Your name is also a major part of your marketing. I'm fairly sure that I could have come up with a more imaginative name but I don't know whether that would have helped my business or not. Consider the message that you want to portray and reflect this in your name. Consider the image that each of these names evokes and decide which style is right for you:

- Hudson & Co
- Hudson Accountants
- Save £££s Accounting
- Revelation Accounting
- Hudson Business Accountants and Advisers

Do listen to non-accountants on this, especially if they are business owners in the group you are likely to be targeting.

You may want more than one domain name for marketing reasons.

Email

Domain names are cheap so there is no excuse not to have a bespoke email address. Using a Hotmail or Gmail address could be seen as particularly unprofessional.

Companies House

If you are the only director/shareholder in your business then you could consider setting up the company yourself directly with Companies House. If there are any other parties involved then you should definitely take legal advice in setting up the company. It is also worth putting in place a shareholder agreement that will define how you will run the company together and the process to follow in the event that you wish to go your separate ways in the future. If you go into business with your best friend then this is the document that should ensure that you stay best friends afterwards too.

It takes 48 hours to set up a limited company online.

Bank accounts

Set up a separate account for your business transactions so that they are not entwined with your personal affairs. If you trade as a limited company then this will need to be in the company name. If you are a sole trader then it can be in your name (I started by using a spare personal account) or the trading name of your business. You may also wish to have a separate deposit account to save for VAT, corporation tax or future expansion plans.

Setting up bank accounts can take a few weeks and has become quite an onerous process. With the new challenger banks such as Tide and Starling this can be done in a matter of minutes.

Having a link with a particular bank will not result in referrals from them.

Telephones

As you can set up a virtual number for anywhere in the world that is easily diverted to wherever you want to receive it, this is not as cumbersome as it used to be. However, you do need to consider how accessible you want to be.

0845/0345/0800 numbers are more expensive for you but they may be useful if you have a niche that will attract a nationwide client base.

A landline will give the impression that you have premises. This is the option I went for when first setting up from home. The same number can follow you around different premises. I would also recommend engaging a professional answering service as soon as you can afford it.

A mobile number suggests that you are available anytime, anywhere. I have always avoided this in order to help maintain a sensible work–life balance. I would suggest that, if you intend to take on staff at any point, you probably want a number they can answer on your behalf as a means of delegation.

Using your existing home line (land or mobile) is out of the question. You will probably want to answer your business and personal calls in a different way.

Answering services can be used to take messages within or outside business hours. They can also be used to provide a virtual receptionist, screening your calls before putting clients through. Some services can combine this with diary management. I would say that, once you've agreed the level of service, it is how well your answering service understands your business which is of most importance.

Practising certificate

An unqualified layperson can set up an accountancy practice without a practising certificate. However, any qualified accountant will have to jump through certain hoops to obtain one. Each professional body is different so get in touch with yours as soon as possible. If you are still training or are newly qualified you will probably have to wait until you have passed all your exams and also have a certain amount of post-qualification experience. There will be a fee to pay to your professional body in addition to your personal subscription. Professional bodies can often offer useful templates and draft policies/procedures, so do make the most of your subscription.

Professional indemnity insurance

This is a requirement of all professional bodies. It is also best practice for any non-qualified professional. Your insurance needs to be in place to cover any advice that you give.

Alternate

Some professional bodies require that, if you are a sole practitioner, you have a named alternate in the event of you being unable to work. Even if this is not essential it is certainly best practice to look after your clients, and you will need to ensure that your family know who to contact. Also consider who should hold power of attorney for your business affairs.

Data protection

If you intend to hold client, employee or contact data then you will have to register your business with the Information Commissioner's Office (ICO). This is fairly simple to do and there is a small admin fee. You obviously have an obligation to keep this data secure. There is a lot of hype about what you actually need to do so take advice on the minimum practical requirements for the size and nature of your business. Essentially you have to document what information you will hold, how and why. You also need to arrange for destruction of old information and how to provide personal information that you hold about an individual should they make a request to see it.

HMRC

You need to register your business with HMRC within three months of commencing trading. You should register a limited company for corporation tax and yourself for self-assessment if you are receiving dividends. For a sole trader or partnership you should register for self-assessment.

VAT registration

Even if you do not expect to reach the limits for compulsory VAT registration you may choose to voluntarily register for the following reasons:

▶ You can reclaim VAT on many purchases thus reducing your costs
▶ You will look like a larger business

If your clients are VAT registered then it will make no difference to them if you are too but, if your clients are smaller or private individuals, you may wish to defer registration until you have to do this. If you expect to need to register in the future then I would suggest adding about 10–20 per cent on to your fees from the beginning to help buffer the transition when you suddenly increase your fees to these non-registered clients by 20 per cent.

Health and safety

Carry out a risk assessment on all aspects of your business and then seek to mitigate these risks as far as possible. Keep a record of this assessment. It could be quite formal or a list of items with the risk and mitigation against each. Review this list regularly and update it as your business grows and changes, for example clients and contacts visiting your office, taking on employees, taking on premises and so on.

Employees

See Chapter 7, 'Building your team'.

Anti-money laundering

If you are a member of a professional body you will need to comply with their anti-money laundering (AML) requirements and they will be able to advise you on this. If you are not a qualified accountant then you should register with HMRC and pay a fee for them to be your supervising body for this. You will need a named person to be responsible for AML and a suitable procedure for checking new clients and checking ongoing ones.

HMRC agent

In order to liaise with HMRC on behalf of your clients you will need to be a registered agent. Once you have registered as an agent you will need to register separately for each tax you will be dealing with. You will then need to be appointed as agent for each individual client by means of form 64-8 (paper or online), providing details for each tax you will deal with for that client.

I have seen many smaller accountants just using the client's own government gateway login but this is not secure for the client.

Other insurances

There are all sorts of insurance that you may need for your business and it is best to take proper advice on this.

▶ Public liability insurance is insufficient for your professional advice but covers most other likely damage done by/to your business. It will also cover injuries to clients and others visiting your premises. A business-from-home insurance policy is relatively cheap and worth having for peace of mind.

- ▶ Home and contents insurance providers should be notified that you are working from home, especially if you see clients, prospects or staff there. I was not required to upgrade my policy until I was seeing over six people per week (including staff) so there was no cost to me before this time.

- ▶ Motor insurance providers should know that you (and your staff) are using your car for business. As an accountant there was no additional cost to me for doing this although there may be an admin fee to amend this mid-year.

- ▶ Employer liability insurance is required as soon as you take on staff. If you provide work experience you may also need to have this in place but check with the school or local authority.

- ▶ Key man insurance will protect your company financially if anything happens to you or other key members of staff. If you are taken ill it could be used to provide an income for you or to pay for another accountant to continue with your workload. You may choose to use savings for this instead, but do remember that your clients are relying on you to complete their work on time, or to notify them otherwise so they can move to a new accountant.

Legal advice

As you grow I would definitely recommend that you take specific legal advice; however, there are some cheap sources to get you started. Your professional body will provide you with templates for client engagement letters although you will probably find that these do not cover every-thing that you would like them to such as unregulated activities. ICAEW also have some contracts for subcontractors as well as 'fit and proper assessments' and confidentiality checklists. They are adding more useful documents all the time.

If you join the Federation of Small Businesses (FSB) then you will have access to their legal templates for your own use (i.e. not to be passed on to clients). These include an assortment of employment contracts as well as other terms and conditions.

Summary of things to do

- ▶ Decide whether to incorporate.
- ▶ Choose a company name and set up at Companies House.
- ▶ Set up business bank account.
- ▶ Purchase domain name.
- ▶ Set up business email.
- ▶ Set up business telephone number.
- ▶ Apply for practising certificate.
- ▶ Apply for professional indemnity insurance.
- ▶ Appoint an alternate.
- ▶ Register with ICO.
- ▶ Register with HMRC for your own taxes.
- ▶ Register with HMRC as tax agent.
- ▶ Register with AML supervising body.
- ▶ Prepare templates for engagement letters, new client information, AML forms and so on.

Chapter 4
Attending networking events and
business shows

Chapter 4 Attending networking events and business shows

Networking is a great way to start and grow your business with relevant leads via people who know a bit about you. It is unlikely to bring instant success. I estimate 6–12 months before it starts to bring in leads although you may get lucky. It took roughly three years for me to start to bring in the best quality leads through networking. I think that you have to be around long enough for people to get to know you and start thinking of you regularly.

Pros of networking

▶ You will meet potential referrers and suppliers as well as prospects.

▶ If you work alone then this could provide you with human contact.

▶ You can make some good relationships that will stand you in good stead for both your business and personal life.

Cons of networking

▶ You will spend a lot of time, not all of which will directly benefit your business.

▶ You will take a while to work out the best networking groups in your area and which ones suit you and your business.

▶ You will drink a lot of coffee (or equivalent) and may begin to feel as though you're eating for a living.

▶ If you are an introvert then this may be quite painful. See the tips below and also Chapter 11, 'Networking through social media'.

How to network effectively

If, like most accountants, you're an introvert there are a few tips to help you to make the most of networking events.

▶ If possible get a guest list in advance. You can identify people you know and people you would like to get to know. Also people you could introduce to each other.

▶ Prepare some simple questions to open a conversation. If the purpose of the event is business networking then feel free to open conversations. Common ones that you may ask or be asked:
  ▷ Have you been to this event before?
  ▷ Are you local/where is your business located?
  ▷ Isn't the weather unusually hot/cold?

- It is commonly accepted that 'givers gain' meaning that helping others and creating introductions for them will reflect well on you. For an introvert it is often easier to talk about other people than about yourself. In helping others they will often want to help you with useful introductions in return.

- Most networking events have a quick round of introductions. Find out in advance if this is the case and how long you have. I have seen them vary from 45 seconds to two minutes. Have this introduction of you and your business prepared in advance, preferably memorised, but I have seen people read them when they were new to networking. Some networking events use timers so watch out for subtle (or not-so-subtle) signals if you are likely to overrun. Do not overrun your allotted time as it is not just rude but also ineffective because your audience will have switched off.

- An elevator spiel is the brief introduction that you would give about yourself and your business if you were to be asked the question during a brief elevator/lift journey.
  - Start with your name and company, 'Hello, I'm Della Hudson of Hudson Business Accountants and Advisers.'
  - Say what you do, 'As the name would suggest we're accountants who work with companies with up to £10 million turnover. We're also business advisers so we can help small businesses to grow too.'
  - Give an example of how you do this, 'We run strategic planning days to help businesses decide where they're going.'
  - Give a call to action, 'If you'd like to see how we help businesses then do come along to our next Money Matters seminar where I will be speaking on X and [guest speaker] will be talking about Y.'
  - Finish with your name and company, 'I'm Della Hudson of Hudson Business Accountants and Advisers.'

- Your slot may be while people are eating or you may be interrupted by waiting staff asking about any dietary requirements so don't be fazed by this.

- If food is involved or juggling of cups then it isn't unusual for me to spill something. I usually take a jacket to cover up any spillage if required.

- Observe the usual courtesies while dining. Don't start eating until everyone else has been served, including those waiting for special dietary meals. Similarly, if your meal is taking a while to come then it is usual to invite others to eat theirs while it is hot.

- ▶ Ladies do watch out for any gentlemen who are waiting for you to sit down before they do likewise. It is rare but I've been caught out a few times standing up and chatting while a poor man is politely waiting for me to take my seat. The middle of a business meeting is not the time to question whether this is a kind or patronising gesture on their part.

- ▶ Don't forget your business cards! I keep boxes everywhere: in each of my bags, in my office, in my car and a few spares in my phone case. Business cards are often handed around the table as you start your elevator spiel. If you would rather not use business cards for any reason you will be making it unusually difficult for people to stay in touch with you.

- ▶ I use SamCard app on my phone to upload business card information directly to my contacts.

- ▶ If you have more than one business just promote one at each event. People are trying to take in a lot of information and like to label you quickly. You can arrange to meet individuals another time to talk about your affairs in more depth.

Which groups are worth attending?

Closed groups

There are many closed networking groups which only admit one member from each profession. The idea of these is that you get to know people and build a network of introducers. They need to understand your business well enough to sell your services to their own contacts. You will want be confident that you will be comfortable introducing other group members to your contacts.

There is usually an annual fee in addition to the weekly or monthly meeting cost. There is probably an obligation to attend a certain percentage of meetings or to arrange for a colleague to cover in your absence. The financial and time commitment means that these need to be very productive for you.

My own feeling is that these sort of groups have spread themselves too thinly so it really depends on the other members of the group as to how effective this is. Do take the opportunity to go along to one or two meetings before you need to commit to joining the group.

Get to know your fellow members so that you can make good quality introductions for each other. This will consist of regular one-to-one meetings over coffee or similar. Remember to look out for leads for your fellow members. When I belonged to one group I estimated that I spent the recommended day a week on the weekly meeting and generating work for others. I left the group before my membership expired as I did not feel that others were putting in the same effort. The quantity and quality of reciprocal leads will depend on the calibre and effort of others in the group as well as what you can do for them.

Open groups

While a good closed group will probably be the most productive for professional service businesses there are also opportunities to meet people at open groups. These are not members only (although there may be discounts for members) so you are only committed to one event at a time.

This type of event is more favoured by start-ups due to the low cost. There is a higher turnover of attendees so you will get to make more contacts but you will actively need to follow up on this as you are not certain of seeing them again at the next meeting.

As there is nothing to stop other attendees being from your own profession you may need to work harder to differentiate yourself from others. I have been one of three accountants on a table of ten before now.

Interest groups

There are groups that revolve around a common interest as well, such as networking walking groups, networking with kids, women's groups and business choirs. Rotary and Lions groups do a lot of charitable work.

You may well find it easier to build strong and trusting relationships when you have worked alongside somebody in this way.

Non-business networks

As well as formal business networks there will be other groups that you are involved in according to your leisure activities or through your family and friends. There may be good connections within these non-business groups.

While these are not overt business networking groups you may find that you are working or training alongside somebody who could be a useful business contact. These relationships deserve to be treated respectfully; people don't necessarily want to talk business while at the gym but it is another source of introductions if handled appropriately.

Follow up

After each event you need some sort of system to follow up. There are plenty of free or cheap customer relationship management (CRM) systems available. It is worth researching to find one which will grow with your business but you can always change later.

Check that you have your new contact's permission to use their details for any particular purpose.

You can send an initial email to those whom you met to invite them to stay in touch either through a regular e-news or a specific meeting such as coffee.

Let's have coffee

This may or may not mean having coffee; personally I drink tea and so do many of my connections (cake or lunch is a good addition), but it is a shorthand invitation to meet up to get to know each other. It is an opportunity to discuss both your businesses and how you can help each other. It may just be that you like each other or it may be that you can see specific business opportunities.

Although this is a great opportunity to strengthen your network you are allowed to say 'no'. Many businesses would love to take advantage of an introduction to your clients. I once had four different independent financial adviser (IFA) firms contact me in a fortnight with similar invitations. Your time is limited but do try to help other people as well as yourself.

The meeting can be at either of your offices or, more comfortably, at a local café. It may be convenient to tag them on to the end of another networking meeting of the same group. This can be quite a useful way to filter out serial networkers who flit from group to group without building real relationships.

Business shows

Pros of exhibiting

▶ Exposure to several businesses all in one place at one time

Cons of exhibiting

▶ Cost of exhibiting together with any giveaways
▶ Time spent exhibiting

How to make the most of a business show

When contemplating exhibiting at a business show you need to be aware of a few things:

- ▶ Who will be attending the show? Go along as an attendee first to see if the right sort of people are there.
- ▶ Although there are usually rules against soliciting when you are an attendee, there are still plenty who will try to go beyond the bounds of their free or cheap ticket. I politely ask if they are exhibiting and then explain the rules if they are not.
- ▶ You need a display and giveaways and sufficient people to man your stand. If the show is busy then you will need one to two people on the stand at all times, and so perhaps a third person to cover breaks. This will allow you to visit the other stands as well as have one-to-one meetings with other exhibitors and attendees.
- ▶ Suggestions for your display and giveaways:
    - ▷ At least one pop-up banner behind the stand so that it is easy for visitors to see who you are
    - ▷ A cloth to cover the table and hide any bags and boxes underneath (also Blu-tack, Sellotape, string and safety pins for fixing everything in place)
    - ▷ A slideshow if you have power
    - ▷ Sweets or similar to draw people to your stand in order for you to talk to them
    - ▷ Literature to give away such as a general brochure about your business (an A4 bifold is relatively cheap) or a specific flyer about your products and services, or helpful information such as tax cards or business cards
    - ▷ Branded goodies to give away such as pens (a good, cheap way to start), mugs or water bottles, notepads or keyrings. Remember that your promotional items are doing nothing to win you new business if they are stuck in a cupboard, so the idea is to give them away. Branded bags are great so that people walk around the show or out of the door displaying your name
- ▶ Make sure that those manning the stand look interested and welcoming all the time. Try not to look at phones on the stand, face outwards and smile even if chatting to each other. Try not to eat on the stand if you have enough people to cover a proper break. If you are on your own then an adjacent stand will usually be happy to look after your stand and enquiries if they are not busy.

- ▶ Collect as many contacts as you can. It is easy to invite someone to join you at an event or to subscribe to your mailing list. Make sure that they are aware of what you will be using their information for and get their specific permission.
- ▶ Follow up after the event as you would any networking event.

Summary

- ▶ Both networking and exhibitions are a good way of getting yourself known amongst local businesses.
- ▶ Find a suitable networking group or event.
- ▶ Make sure that you know the format of networking meetings.
- ▶ Prepare your brief verbal introduction of your business.
- ▶ Have plenty of business cards for networking and other promotional goods to give away at events.
- ▶ Have plenty of manpower to cover your stand at events.
- ▶ Follow up to make the most of the contacts you have made.

Chapter 5
Setting your prices

Unless you are a charity then your business needs to make a certain amount of money to cover direct costs, wages, other overheads and an amount for you. Your personal profit target is probably more than you would want for the same number of hours as an employee as you are bearing all sorts of additional risks beyond those of a normal nine to five with a guaranteed pay cheque.

Pros of proper pricing

The income that you generate in your own business allows you to do three things:

▶ Financial freedom is the obvious one. If you were to replace yourself with an employee doing the same work at a commercial salary would there still be any profit? If not, this is self-employment rather than a business. It may be that self-employment is all that you want or it may be a step on the way to growing an independent business. Yes, there was a point when I was in this situation too on the way to scaling my business. Earning money for ourselves is usually a major motivation in setting up a business, so let's do it well.

▶ Quality and pride. If you want to provide a service or product of which you can be proud then you need to be able to spend sufficient time to put in the work required. Do you feel as though all the work you produce is top quality? How often do you rush to complete a job because it is just haemorrhaging cash and time? Only do work that you can be pleased to acknowledge as your own.

▶ Time freedom. If you do not charge enough to pay someone to do the work it is often the business owner who puts in the extra hours to complete the job. Proper pricing will pay for time, either personal time or time to grow your business.

Cons of proper pricing

▶ Losing clients who can't or won't pay the necessary fee

Issues to consider

▶ Market price and where you sit in the market
▶ Value to your client

- ▶ Cost to you (including a share of overheads and your own profit element)
- ▶ How to increase your prices

Price and your competitors

When you first set up in business you usually set your price somewhere in line with your competitors as if this is the market price for the service that you provide without differentiating yourself to justify a different price.

Cost-based pricing is the hourly charging of traditional accountants with no reward for efficiency or automation. Carrying out a similar job will be faster the second time so it would be unfair to penalise one client for your learning curve or to undercharge another. Although many accountants still charge this way it is less common now for these reasons.

One thing that is clear is that you cannot compete on price against the big corporations that 'pile them high and sell them cheap'. These companies have purchasing power and economies of scale which you cannot hope to match. You can probably not compete with the small businesses based at home that have minimal overheads. Competitor businesses below the VAT threshold can sell to the public or non-VAT registered clients who cannot reclaim VAT without the 20 per cent VAT premium.

Price and quality

What you can compete on is quality or value for money.

Thinking of your typical client how long does it take you to do a fairly standard job of average quality? How much would you charge for that particular job?

Now consider how much more it would take to provide a Wow! kind of job. How much could you charge? How much extra would it cost? How would people compare this to your competitors?

When new clients came to me and complained that they were not getting the kind of service that they wanted from their accountant, the first thing I did was to ask how much they were paying. My question was usually along the lines of 'how can you expect the service that you describe for that fee?'

It is rare to get extraordinary value at the cheap end of the market. The most extreme example was somebody who was paying £50 per year to a family friend and expected monthly management accounts for that price. A job that we would price at a few thousand pounds! As she was a small one-man band, that price was not realistic for her but neither was her need for monthly accounts. We agreed on a realistic price and service for her business and told her which key numbers to monitor each month.

If new prospects generally got along with their accountant but felt that they weren't getting what they wanted from them, we would usually suggest that they negotiate a different service and probably a higher fee. Some still preferred to come to us as they felt that their accountant couldn't provide the required service. This is a warning to make sure that existing clients know all the services that you offer so that they don't need to start looking elsewhere.

Even with something as simple as conveyancing, which is a fairly standard job and, on the face of it, doesn't need a qualified solicitor, you might benefit from paying a little more. We bought a bulk standard ten-year-old estate house without a mortgage and decided to use one of the cheap conveyancing firms. When we came to sell we used a proper solicitor as the matter was more complex because we were buying another property and there was a mortgage involved. We discovered that our buyers' solicitors were much more thorough than our original conveyancers had been. We ended up having to pay for insurance as there was information that we were unable to provide because our conveyancer had never requested it from our original vendors.

Increasing your prices

Many people worry that by putting up their prices they may lose business, but let me show you an example.

If you have 100 sales of £1,000 each and an associated cost of £500 (so £500 profit) you might choose to increase your prices by 10 per cent to £1,100.

Now, instead of an income of £100,000 and profit of £50,000 you would have income of £110,000 and profit of £60,000.

If you lose 10 per cent of your clients through this 10 per cent price increase you would have 90 clients paying £1,100 each and so an income of £99,000 and profit of £54,000. You have increased your profit by £4,000 while having more time to do a good job for fewer clients.

With this example you could afford to lose 17 per cent of your customers and still make the same profit but you would be ahead on the processing costs because you are handling fewer transactions.

As an added bonus your most price sensitive customers are probably those who cause you the most trouble. You probably have your own example of where you have been squeezed on profit and the client was still not satisfied.

Negotiating prices

When you first set up in business you are often feeling your way on pricing. After a while you know what you are worth, although people sometimes still try to negotiate beyond this.

You could have your starting prices on your website, or at least a printed price list for your own reference so that you do not quote unrealistic prices when put on the spot.

It also helps to package your services. Clients can choose the service package that suits them but the price for each package is fixed. When I have been asked for a cheaper price I have helped the client to decide what they can do for themselves to reduce their costs, such as some basic bookkeeping. If they do not wish to change the services then I have to explain that we are unable to provide a level of service that we can be proud of for any less. Sometimes we have to let prospective clients go because we cannot do what they want, to a standard that we want for the fee that they can afford. There are plenty of other accountants out there and I've sometimes even been able to refer business to my competitors.

Turning away the wrong business

If you find that you have a lot of enquiries that are not the right client for you, then it is worth building relationships with others who may be looking for exactly that type of business. For instance we did not take on new clients who had left things until the last minute. If clients cannot prioritise their accountancy then they are depriving themselves of an essential tool to grow their business. Our expertise was helping businesses to grow: we could only help them, we couldn't do it for them if they were not serious about their own business.

Of course we made an exception for a client who was late because he had been diagnosed with cancer and we pulled out all the stops to ensure that everything was completed on time so that he did not incur penalties.

Deciding your price

So, how do you determine what your services are worth?

I once wrote a single letter to HMRC which took no particular research and saved a client £2,400 in tax. The admin that I had to complete, in line with

ICAEW guidelines, in order to take on the client actually took longer than writing the letter.

So what do you think I should have charged?

a) £100 as the notional cost of my time to write the letter

b) £300 as the cost of my time to speak to the client, carry out all the necessary new client admin including money laundering checks for HMRC and then the time to write the actual letter (this was a one-off piece of work)

c) £800 as the client would still be better off by £1,600 if the appeal was successful

d) Not a fixed fee but 50 per cent of any tax saving

Was the client paying for my time or my expert qualification and 20+ years of experience that allowed me to write the quick letter? Why do accountants and other professionals charge by the hour?

Think about how you set your fees.

Presenting your prices

There has been a great deal of research showing that if you present three models of increasing price and quality, people will often avoid the cheapest as they do not wish to be seen as 'cheap'.

You could have bronze, silver and gold packages. Does anybody have an ordinary Barclaycard these days? Even my entry level card, which is never used, is a platinum card.

Warning

If you increase your prices without giving value for money then you will end up losing business and reputation, so do not promise what you cannot fulfil.

My favourite client reference was: 'You are more expensive than [another local accountant] but much easier to deal with.'

I like it because it shows that we got our pricing right on this one and the client appreciated that we were giving value for money. We used this quote in our marketing for a while.

Annual increases

Don't forget that your costs are going up and that your clients' businesses are growing and changing too. Make time to review your client list each year to ensure that everybody is receiving the services that they need and discuss additional (or no longer necessary) services with your client. You should also have a standard inflationary increase to cover your own costs and it is worth having this included in your engagement letter.

Overcharging or underservicing?

Have you ever been sitting in a restaurant waiting for your meal and fancied another drink? This happened to me recently and the server was nowhere to be seen, so I was left sitting, thirsty and noticing the lack of service and the long wait for food.

Although it may sometimes be irritating to be cross-sold extras, it was probably more infuriating to be without the drink that I wanted, which also led me to notice faults that I would otherwise have overlooked. As well as losing out on about 21 per cent extra sales, the restaurant had an unhappy customer who may well go elsewhere next time.

You don't need a hard sell but do ensure that clients are aware of additional services that you think may be of use to them.

Avoiding pitfalls

If you are worried about a generic price increase or don't know what you're worth, then you can phase in an increase by starting with new clients. Then just increase prices for a few existing clients each month.

Don't be afraid of losing poor clients.

Summary

- ▶ You are in business to make money not to provide a charitable service.
- ▶ There is nothing wrong with being paid what you are worth.
- ▶ Charge enough to provide the level of service that your client expects and deserves.
- ▶ Quality commands a higher fee but do make sure that you fulfil your promises.
- ▶ Try bundling your services into packages.
- ▶ Increase all your fees annually.
- ▶ Don't be afraid to increase your fees if they are too low.

Chapter 6
Budgeting and controlling costs

My background includes working as a financial controller in large companies and I am a great believer in cost control rather than blind cost cutting.

There are times when it is right to go through a bootstrapping, cost constrained period, for instance in the start-up phase when money is tight. This works because you have more time as you have fewer customers to service. Once your time has become a precious commodity, it is time to take a fresh look and see what it will really take to grow your business. I don't want you to waste your money but I do know that one way to pretty much guarantee a business failure is to stop investing in it.

Cost control

This is about spending money as an investment in the growth of your company. It might be paying for software to reduce time-consuming manual processes. The focus is on value not absolute cost.

Cost reduction aka bootstrapping

This is about cutting spending to the bare minimum. It is about making do with what you can afford now, although you may end up paying more at a future date to replace or upgrade.

We went from a DIY website to a £500 site to a £3,000 site. I believe that each was worth the money that we spent but, by starting out with a DIY site, we learned a few new skills and were able to save cash for things that we couldn't do at all. This was not a productive use of time but time was not the most limited resource at first. It was also a good learning experience.

A downside of this cost cutting mentality is that business founders often get into the habit of doing things themselves instead of paying an expert to do it for them cheaper, faster and/or better.

Here are a few ideas on controlling your costs.

People costs

- ▶ Recruit a part-timer
- ▶ Recruit somebody junior and cheap who will take more time
- ▶ Recruit somebody senior who can do the job fast and well even though their hourly rate may be higher
- ▶ Outsource the activity

Recruit for the work that you need and don't be obsessed with padding it out to provide a full-time role which might require two or three different skill sets. There are all sorts of reasons that people might be looking for part-time work. In my experience the school gates are full of highly qualified mothers (mainly) who would kill for a job that used their skills and still allowed them to be available for their children. Our local post office employed two mothers who were economics and marketing graduates and my old cleaner had a Master of Business Administration (MBA). You could be employing one of these for a few hours a week or even a month. This is ideal for smaller companies which can't afford to pay for the level of expertise that they need, nor do they have the need for a full-time person in this role. It isn't just mothers who need this flexibility so keep an open mind.

You can provide flexibility in hours but also in location. We ran on a remote desktop so our team could work from anywhere in the world provided there was an Internet connection. As all our staff were office based it meant that they could work through snow, floods and children's illnesses or even because they wanted to be at home with a new puppy.

Talking of which, we used to have dogs in the office (once the puppy was housetrained!). These are little things that make people happy and don't actually cost you any money. If you can't trust your team to work unsupervised at least part of the time, then I would question whether they are the right people for your business.

Another way to get flexibility is to outsource. I have used a virtual PA where I only paid for the hours worked. We used an outsourced answering service to cover when our team were out of the office, in meetings or on the phone. Naturally clients used us to outsource their bookkeeping and payroll so that they could focus on what they were best at. We could do the same work better and faster than most of them. You will often find this when you delegate to experts. This is one of the reasons that we opted for a hosted desktop; it was backed up, kept secure and maintained by experts leaving me free to do what I was best at which was growing my business and helping clients to do the same.

The key to using human resources internally or externally is to organise your business into systems.

1. Identify your systems starting with the most repetitive.
2. Write the procedure.
3. Can you simplify it?
4. Can you automate it?
5. Can you delegate it to someone cheaper or more expert?

Consider temporary staff for project work or to help you during busy periods, rather than keeping a larger permanent workforce. Zero hours contracts have been abused by some larger businesses but they are a good alternative for regular temps, giving them employment rights that they would not have otherwise.

Get the right contracts in place. Members of the FSB have access to a selection of standard HR contracts and procedures or, for something more complex, speak to a proper HR solicitor, which could save you a fortune at a later date.

Premises

For many people premises is a large part of their overhead budget. Leases can seem very inflexible for a rapidly expanding business. If you're going to double your workforce in three to five years, then do you want to pay today for the bigger offices to save the hassle of moving to larger premises at a later date?

Again, for growing businesses, flexibility is the key. Serviced offices are ideal as you can swiftly move into a small office with instant utilities, Internet and telecoms infrastructure. The most common of these is Regus but there are also many independents that can offer a better service or price.

As your business grows you can take on a second office in the same building, have two smaller offices opened out into one or move along the corridor without changing address. This is, of course, subject to your building having sufficient growing-on space available at the same time that you need it, so do think ahead.

Serviced offices can also provide a full-time receptionist, photocopiers, printers and PA services at an additional cost.

Don't forget that, if you decide to purchase your own commercial premises, these can be wrapped up in a tax-efficient self-invested pension plan (SIPP) to provide the business owner with a future pension.

Marketing: investment or overhead?

Marketing is often a large budget item for a growing business. One of the classic quotes is that 50 per cent of marketing works but the difficulty is knowing which 50 per cent. This is where it pays to use an expert to help you put the right strategy in place.

Marketing is shown as an overhead but do record how effective each campaign and method is for you. Things like social media can appear to be free but are actually quite time-consuming to get the best out of them, so do value your time as this becomes more limited. Bootstrappers (start-ups with minimal resources) need to invest time in marketing to make up for their lack of cash.

Different types of marketing will have different times to return a benefit and, as a new business, it is best to invest in a mixture to generate clients now and in the future.

You can find marketing consultants to advise you on what will be most effective for your business and its aims, and you can find experts who will actually run the campaigns for you. I used a mixture of my own copy as well as buying in some material because I didn't have the time to generate enough content myself. Web content needs to be original for search engine optimisation (SEO) purposes so I write this myself. I can't add value to a tax card full of numbers so I just pay somebody else to produce this for me, just as I pay somebody to write and maintain our tax app. I don't have time to learn more technology when I'm busy keeping up with the constantly changing tax and company law.

Technology

Which brings us on to IT where there are many decisions to be made.

IT decision 1 – automated or manual

I describe myself as a competent user and I spent three years supporting and maintaining the accounting systems at National Grid. If I had all the time in the world I could have learned about each of our systems in-depth and maintained them myself but my business was accountancy, not getting bogged down in the nitty-gritty of servers and coding websites. We were in the business of helping businesses to grow, so spending my time with my nose under the bonnet of a computer would not have helped my clients.

In my bootstrapping days I did tax calculations on spreadsheets that I had written myself. With hindsight, even then, I should have purchased tax software so that I could spend more time adding value for clients. I would always recommend automating repetitive or complex jobs so that you work on that which only you can do. See Chapter 2, 'Establishing your systems and services' for more ideas. The time saved for you to focus on your business will pay for itself in results elsewhere.

IT decision 2 – integrated or best of breed

Do you buy cheap software separately for each part of your work or do you buy a single integrated package? Xero, Taxcalc and Sage are all moving towards an element of integration with tax and practice management but, in my opinion, they aren't there yet. We chose to use separate software for tax, accounting, bookkeeping, CRM and workflows. Most of them talked to each other but there was a certain amount of duplicate input that we accepted in exchange for having the 'best of breed' of each type of software. Other accountants opt for a single system that can do everything, even though the overall standard is not as good and, usually, the price is higher. You will need to make similar decisions about your business software.

IT decision 3 – market leader or cheaper

Our business had standardised on Microsoft Office but I know others that prefer OpenOffice as a money saving exercise in spite of the inefficiencies. There is a time cost in making this less well known software integrate with some systems.

IT decision 4 – cloud or server

We used cloud-based software wherever available and a hosted desktop for everything else. Our server was somewhere in the country with a failover elsewhere. We paid a monthly fee for the server and an expert team to maintain it. We did not have the huge capital outlay to purchase our own server and backup server and did not need to worry about when to replace them. We didn't need to worry about software upgrades, backups or security. Having worked in disaster recovery I was quite happy to let the experts deal with this.

If our Internet connection failed for any reason then we had the option of working elsewhere. As our PCs were dumb terminals (you may remember these if you've used an old mainframe) there was no data lost if somebody stole one.

This is the reason that we recommended Xero software for clients who use their own bookkeeper. This is cloud-based software that can be accessed from anywhere and you can invoice, log expenses and log time from your smartphone while out and about. We worked with all sorts of cloud software if necessary but Xero was definitely our overall favourite.

IT decision 5 – software or you

We had workflow software to track jobs through the business. The idea of our workflow software was that anyone could see what was happening with any client at any point in time. It made me replaceable, as basic knowledge was not held in my head. If your business runs independently of the owner it is a saleable commodity and can be part of your pension plan.

IT essential – disaster recovery

On the subject of disaster recovery I strongly suggest that you write out your contingency plan in the event that your PC becomes corrupted or stolen, or your Internet connection or telecoms fail. We kept a paper list of all IT and communications contacts on the office wall as it would be no good held electronically if the system had failed.

If you are dependent on your PCs, then I recommend looking into a maintenance contract that will cover you for emergency work or for routine upgrades and other odd problems. You can opt for an ongoing contract or pay as you go. The latter will be more expensive but you only pay when you have a problem.

Avoiding pitfalls

If you cut costs far enough the business will be unable to function and so will fail.

There is an opportunity cost to bootstrapping. You may not be able to take advantage of an opportunity if you do not have sufficient funds to invest. In other words 'you have to be in it to win it'.

There is also a cost involved in shopping around to save pennies when you could be earning far more out there doing what you are best at.

Summary

- ▶ Costs are also an investment in your business.
- ▶ An expert should be able to do things cheaper, faster and/or better than you can.
- ▶ Consider part-time or outsourcing work.
- ▶ Consider different ways of paying for technology up front or as a service.
- ▶ Consider pay as you go versus maintenance contracts.
- ▶ Please consider all your overheads as an investment as well as a cost.

Chapter 7
Building your team

If you want to grow your business you need more resources than a single person, even if you are prepared to put in long hours. If you want a saleable business you will also need to demonstrate that it operates independently of you. Once you've made the decision to grow the business beyond the work of one person, the main decision to make is whether to outsource (and how) or to employ.

Pros of growing beyond a one-man band

- ▶ Provides you with income even when you're not working
- ▶ Allows you access to expertise beyond your own
- ▶ Helps you to develop a more saleable business which operates independently of you
- ▶ Opportunity to delegate the jobs you are not so keen on!
- ▶ Reduced interaction with clients

Cons of growing beyond a one-man band

- ▶ Managing other people may not be your forte
- ▶ Managing people takes time
- ▶ You may require bigger premises
- ▶ Difficulty finding the right people
- ▶ What if you take on the wrong person?
- ▶ Reduced interaction with clients

Issues to consider

- ▶ What level of knowledge or experience do you require?
- ▶ How many hours per week do you require?
- ▶ Do you need additional space for them to work? Desk? PC?
- ▶ How much time will it take to train them (even for a competent, qualified accountant)?
- ▶ How will you cope with the busy interim period while you are trying to train your new starter and do your own work?
- ▶ What funding or grants are available for training and other costs?
- ▶ Where is the best place to advertise?

- ▶ If this is your first employee, will you need a network or will you share IT systems?
- ▶ You will need employers' liability insurance.

Finding the right person

I have always said that I would rather stay small than take on the wrong person. When a key member of staff left and I failed to find a suitable replacement we did have a clear-out of clients.

As a small business owner you want to get the most out of any advert in the local paper. A small box can include your logo, a few job details including salary and a link to your website. This then doubles up as a marketing exercise. The full details of the vacancy are on your website. Decide what is absolutely necessary to the role that you cannot do without and what skills your ideal candidate would hold. These are the things that you will and won't compromise on when sorting CVs and then interviewing. You might want to specify a qualification 'or equivalent experience' to broaden the field.

Remember to regularly post the job link on all your social media accounts.

Consider using online job boards. Free or cheap online job boards make it so easy for the candidate to press a button and apply that they are tempted to apply for roles for which they are clearly not suitable. You may receive more applications this way but you will also waste a lot of time filtering through unsuitable CVs.

Advertise for a couple of weeks before printing off all suitable CVs. Note on these CVs whether to interview or reasons for rejection in case of future enquiries. I always emailed rejections and wished them all the best. It's hard hanging on wondering when or if they'll hear from you so be kind to everybody you deal with.

I did not use agencies. There may be some good ones out there but there were also some truly poor ones and it was hard to tell the difference until too late. This was learned from my own experience on both sides of the interview table.

Work experience

We offered work experience to local schools. While the young ones were there to learn about office life or because the school was making them do something, we found that sixth formers were more likely to be considering a career in accountancy. They were also able to carry out some useful work and to converse better than younger students when introduced to clients and other business colleagues. This could act as an extended interview if we were thinking of recruiting.

If you work with schools then careers fairs and mock interviews are another good way to identify potential recruits early on.

Subcontractors

Personally I preferred to employ regular workers so that it was clear that they had employment rights and to help them feel that they belonged to the team. When I acquired a bookkeeping practice, there were three sub-contractors and one of them chose to come onto the payroll. Employees are entitled to paid holiday and other statutory leave and you will need to pay pensions and national insurance in addition to their salary, so they are usually paid slightly less than subcontractors.

Do be clear about the employment status of any subcontractors. Ensure that you take up references, confirm any qualifications and check that they have professional indemnity insurance. The ICAEW website has standard contracts for subcontractors as well as a confidentiality agreement.

Apprentices

My first employee was an apprentice. I had wavered between a part-time qualified accountant who would hit the ground running and a full-time apprentice whom I would have to train but who could be trained in exactly the way I wanted things done. The deciding factor was having somebody around to answer the phone when I was out. It worked very well because my apprentice was on day release during term time but in the office for the full five days when I wanted more time with my kids.

Taking on an apprentice allowed me to pay a lower salary, which was the only way that I could afford to grow my business. It also meant that I could afford to set aside 12-months' salary in my deposit account to ensure that I would have enough to at least train him through one year of AAT. Beware, under the apprentice scheme there was plenty of paperwork and, with subsequent apprentices, this has increased threefold. For the first apprentice the college came and helped me with the paperwork to enrol him on the course and to help with funding. The course was partly funded itself (as he was over 18) and also a one-off grant which I put towards a desk, chair, laptop and software licenses.

Accountancy training has traditionally followed a mixture of theory and in-house training so the apprentice scheme is ideally suited to accountancy trainees. AAT courses are widely available and the college may even be able to help you with recruitment.

Induction

A proper induction procedure will help your new recruits to hit the ground running on day one. Taking them out for lunch on their first day will help the team to get to know each other better and help your new recruit feel extra welcome.

Useful items for your induction checklist are:

- ▶ Add them to the tea/coffee list with their personalised mug (priorities!)
- ▶ Toilet facilities, door codes and so on
- ▶ Employment contract, fit and proper form for ICAEW, confidentiality contract
- ▶ Payroll details – P45/6, proof of ID, next of kin, bank details
- ▶ Desk, chair, PC and stationery all ready beforehand
- ▶ PC and software logins (make sure that these are set up before the start date)
- ▶ Admin procedures, for example telephones, post in/out, filing of paper and online, expenses, visitors and client visits
- ▶ HR procedures, for example holiday, sickness
- ▶ Discuss one page plan and team key performance indicators (KPIs)
- ▶ Client list
- ▶ Basic software training – often via video, for example Xero certification

Contracts

You must provide your employees with a contract. If you are a member of FSB you will have access to all sorts of contracts to use in-house free of charge. As these contracts are constantly updated do ensure that you are using the latest version for new recruits. It may be more appropriate for you to consult an employment solicitor for more senior staff or for anything unusual.

Your governing body may require additional checks. The ICAEW website has a 'fit and proper person' declaration which the team complete each year as well as a separate confidentiality contract.

Our contracts all had a three-month probationary period. If you do find that you have recruited the wrong person then it is least painful all round to acknowledge the mistake sooner rather than later. Dismissing somebody is a horrible thing to do so ensure that you carry it out legally, according to your procedures, document everything, and do it as kindly as possible. You are in control of the situation so be clear and be considerate. FSB membership includes access to employment law advice but you may wish to consult your own employment solicitor.

Part-time/flexible

The beauty of accountancy work is that it needn't be confined to specific hours. You may choose to have core hours or to require a minimum number in the office at any time but it is also possible to operate completely remotely. I know one practice that employs a qualified accountant who happens to live in Australia.

All our team had specified days/hours based in the office but were free to switch those hours or work from home by prior arrangement. This flexibility worked to our advantage at busy times when staff would hang on to finish a job knowing that they wouldn't lose out as they could take extra holiday at a quieter time to suit themselves.

Any additional hours worked, at evening events for example, were generally compensated by time off in lieu. This is because it is important that people have time for family and outside interests. When this was not possible during a period when we were recruiting then the overtime was paid instead.

If you're not sure how many hours you will require then a zero hours contract could be the thing for you. These have received bad press where they have obliged the employee to be available for work but, if obligations are reciprocal, they can be much fairer. You have no obligation to provide work but your employee has no obligation to be available, so you may prefer to specify a minimum number of hours. Essentially your employee will have employment rights but any financial aspects will be based on average hours worked.

If your team operate remotely or part-time then communication is key. We allocated clients to different team members so they and others could use our CRM to note important matters for everybody to see. Our CRM also held a copy of all email correspondence to/from the client, although this required a certain discipline in changing the email subject line whenever the subject changed in an email chain.

We found that offering flexible working gave us access to some high-calibre women whose hours were constrained by young children. They were complemented by semi-retired staff who wanted long weekends but not school holidays. The only downside was that we ended up with a predominantly female team while I would have preferred a more diverse mix. As a small business this was unavoidable, but increased diversity is something that you might aspire to in order to bring fresh ideas and viewpoints into your business.

Looking after your team

I am a great believer that if you look after your team, they will look after your clients. I once heard that it is more important to look after your employees as, with the right team, it is easy to find new clients. Treat your staff as you want them to treat your best clients.

We held annual appraisals in order to have a formal conversation to document plans, ambitions and training requirements for the coming year. These should never be a substitute for good communication throughout the year but serve as an opportunity to ensure that your people's personal ambitions and those of the business are aligned. If people have aspirations beyond what is possible in the business then it is best not to attempt to hold them back but to help them find a role elsewhere which will satisfy their requirements. If the individual is no longer suitable for your growing and changing business then you will need to provide retraining or even help them to move on.

Some of our team were focusing on their families or, for other reasons, had no career ambitions. We changed their appraisal forms to read job ambitions rather than career ambitions so that we could give them the support they needed to flourish.

If you struggle with appraisals then you will be pleased to hear that these can be outsourced to a specialist such as Smart Support for Business.

Training

For trainees there is a clear training path with external college through day release or home study. As far as possible try to have a structure to your internal, on the job, training. For qualified staff you will need to arrange continuing professional development (CPD). We used a mixture of 2020 online courses, other webinars and face-to-face events. Xero provide excellent online training and free annual roadshows as well as Xerocon, the annual two-day Xero conference and party.

The annual Accountex exhibition in London provides a large number of seminars suitable for CPD and other learning. It is also worth visiting for an opportunity to meet software and other suppliers in person.

Providing good training may enable staff to leave you but, frankly, why would they want to leave if you are treating them well and encouraging their personal aspirations? There may be times when the nature of the business does not allow you to provide opportunities for your best staff at the right moment but, by encouraging your team to follow their own ambitions when they no longer align with yours, you will still have a reputation as a good employer.

Personality profiles

For many accountants people are incomprehensible. Treating people as we would like to be treated doesn't always work. One way of understanding them better is to use DISC profiles. These, and other types of personality profiles, attempt to broadly categorise people in order to give an idea of how we each work best. We profiled the whole team and shared the reports, including mine, so that we could understand what made each of us 'tick' and how to get the best out of each other. There are some accountants who also do this for their clients to ensure that they communicate in the best way.

Organisation chart

An organisation chart shows all the roles within your business from the managing director to the receptionist. Michael Gerber (2001), in his *E-Myth* book, suggests that you draw one up from the beginning. Initially you will be doing every job on your organisation chart and your first team member will probably take on the simplest of the technical work, or perhaps the marketing and admin. As your organisation grows, each person will start to have discrete job roles and the organisation will move from a single team to multiple teams. There are various ways that you can evolve your structure:

- ▶ By function, for example separate admin, accounting, bookkeeping, and tax teams
- ▶ By client, for example a client manager will be responsible for everything to do with particular clients

Some companies have separate cloud departments dealing exclusively with clients on cloud-based software systems as they see this new technology as a specialist skill but, in a modern firm, cloud will be used by all your team and probably doesn't justify a separate discipline except, perhaps, for the initial set-up and migration period.

Outsourcing

An alternative to recruiting is outsourcing. This can be done locally to an individual or offshore.

Pros of outsourcing

▶ Increased capacity

▶ Flexible capacity

▶ You are not directly responsible for staff

Cons of outsourcing

▶ Reduced control over quality

▶ Need for quality checks

▶ Data protection and other confidentiality considerations

▶ Works best with clean/simple jobs

Issues to consider

▶ Do you want to outsource to an individual subcontractor or to a company?

▶ How many hours per week/month do you require?

▶ What level of supervision/checking will they need (probably working to the standard of a semi-senior)?

▶ What sort of interim period should you allow while you are each learning how the other works?

▶ Do you want a UK outsourcer or are you happy with one based overseas?

▶ Will you need to share IT systems?

▶ How will you safeguard confidentiality and data protection?

▶ Outsourcing works best with simpler jobs so how will you manage your messier ones?

The process

When a member of staff left and I couldn't find a suitable replacement, I took the opportunity to pass on some of the smaller clients who were no longer suited to us. In spite of this we still had more work than our existing team could handle, so I looked into outsourcing to a firm of chartered accountants in Northern Ireland.

This meant that we shared the same standards but, although wages were slightly lower in Northern Ireland, we made no real margin on the work we outsourced. I chose the company as I wanted to keep the work as local as possible, plus they offered more flexibility in the number of sets of accounts that they would handle for us. The process worked very well on the clean accounts but we did not attempt to outsource any messy jobs because of the extended communication chain.

I checked that our engagement letters allowed us to outsource. For Sage clients we uploaded a backup via their File Transfer Protocol (FTP) link and for cloud clients we gave consultants read only access. They used our Xero Working Papers and produced the final accounts on their own VT Software (the same software as us) but we decided to do the tax in-house as it would allow us to review at the same time.

I was very happy with the outcome but we did not continue this as, in choosing to keep the work as close to home as possible, there was little margin. I would do it again as a short-term measure when unable to take on the right in-house staff.

Self-care

It's not just your team who need looking after. As their leader it is often easy to forget that you need to be in good health, both mentally and physically.

▶ Take some sort of regular exercise. Running suits me best as it can fit around my varying schedule. Running is the only time when nobody else is demanding a piece of me and some days it is my only 'me time'. As it is a fairly repetitive action it provides good thinking time and allows my thoughts to become clearer so that I can often come up with solutions to problems that have been baffling me for days.

▶ Eating well is easier said than done on days where you have lots of business meals out or skip meals while rushing from one meeting to another. Useful snacks to carry are bananas, baby bel cheeses, dried fruit and bread sticks. I usually have an emergency cereal bar in my handbag but these are quite sugary.

▶ Sleeping well should be possible even when running a business. If you work a nightshift because of a deadline do schedule some recovery time. If your mind is racing at bedtime, then keep a pen and pad at your bedside to note thoughts and ideas before settling down to sleep. I often read business books in bed which stimulate ideas at just the wrong time. If you are regularly sleep deprived as a result of business worries, then you need to seek business advice or even consider becoming an employee again.

While staff and clients are dependent on you performing at your best, you have a duty to look after yourself in order to look after them.

Pitfalls to avoid

- ▶ If you make a poor recruitment decision, correct it as quickly as you can but ensure that you do this both legally and kindly.
- ▶ Do not recruit the wrong person in desperation. It is better to stay little and good, so look at internal efficiencies or your client mix instead.
- ▶ Communication is key throughout the year and during annual appraisals.
- ▶ Do ensure that you follow a proper recruitment process and have all the legals in place in the event of any future problems or misunderstandings.

Summary

- ▶ Once you decide to grow beyond a single person you will need to spend some time managing people, so this is not for everyone.
- ▶ You will need to find the right person and provide some level of induction.
- ▶ You may choose to recruit a trainee and the National Apprenticeship Service can help to finance AAT courses.
- ▶ Recruit wisely and look after your team well while staying the right side of all the legalities.
- ▶ If you make a mistake then rectify it rather than let your business suffer.
- ▶ Consider part-time workers rather than wait until you have a full-time vacancy.
- ▶ You can choose between employment and outsourcing.
- ▶ Look after yourself too!

Chapter 8
Choosing your software

Technology is changing rapidly so this chapter gives a method of choosing software rather than information about any single piece of software. Having the right software can really accelerate the growth of your business.

Although I never considered us to be ultra-modern we were often described as early adopters of some of the software. The rate of change is now slowing while others catch up and we wait for the next big step change. One thing is certain, change is constant.

Every time I replaced a manual process with software I wished that I had done it 12 months earlier so, after a while, I just started to adopt software as quickly as it became available. I have always embraced technology so please use my end point as a start point for your business.

Pros of automating

▶ Saves reinventing the wheel on standard processes and calculations

▶ Saves processing time

▶ Tax changes and so on are automatically updated

▶ Moving towards being paperless improves the facility for home/remote working and the security of data

Cons of automating

▶ Cost

▶ Dependence on technology if you are not comfortable with it

Issues to consider

▶ Cost versus time saved

▶ PC or network versus cloud

▶ Ease of use

▶ Ease of support

▶ Training available

▶ A single, integrated system or the best of breed

▶ Data conversion

▶ Security of system and data

Areas to consider

The main areas for which you will need to consider software for your business are:

- ▶ Accounts production
- ▶ Tax returns and calculations
- ▶ Workflow management, that is, ensuring that you don't miss deadlines
- ▶ Bookkeeping
- ▶ Payroll and CIS (Construction Industry Scheme)

Additional areas for the smooth running of the business

- ▶ Online signatures
- ▶ Online data storage or processing
- ▶ Word processing, spreadsheets, presentations, emails

Additional software that could be helpful

- ▶ Management accounts information
- ▶ Optical character recognition for uploading paper or PDF bank statements (when clients can't manage to send you a comma-separated values (CSV) file or similar)
- ▶ Various add-ons to speed up bookkeeping entry

Table 1 contains a list of the main software that we used and why we chose it, along with notes on what we would do differently with more recent changes.

Table 1: Main Software

Software	Function	Main details	Latest developments
VT Accounts	Accounts production	Simple, cheap and Excel based. Cheap add on for charity templates. PC based. iXBRL format and uploads to Companies House	I would consider something like Taxcalc accounts production as an integrated solution. My preference would always be for a true cloud solution.

Software	Function	Main details	Latest developments
*Xero ledger	Working papers	Free to Xero accountants. Provides a single place for all working papers and generates professional looking supporting documents. Integrates with Xero or input a closing trial balance (TB) into Xero ledger.	I still haven't found a better replacement.
Taxcalc	*All tax returns: corporation tax, self-assessment, trust taxes	Simple and cheap	I still haven't found a better replacement but, although the data can be cloud based, the software itself must sit on a PC.
Logical Office and Trello	Workflow management	CRM system holds standing data. Automatically tracks all emails to and from clients, which saves unnecessary cc'ing. It can be used for document management. Comes with templates and workflows for accountants. PC based. The downside is that it is PC based and you pay a subscription and for updates. There is no dashboard so Trello provides a cloud-based dashboard with a single view of all work in progress. We used it rather like the old, manual T-card systems.	This is an area with lots of new entrants expected soon. Xero, Xero Practice Manager (Workflow Max) and Taxcalc all offer elements of this, but I haven't yet found anything which offers as much functionality as Logical Office.

Software	Function	Main details	Latest developments
*Xero (commonly with Receipt Bank)	Bookkeeping	The best all-rounder with plenty of add-ons to make this the financial hub of a business system. The bank feeds and Receipt Bank make it profitable to offer bookkeeping services on a fixed-fee basis with the added benefit of faster, simpler year ends.	Comes with online training for accountants and clients plus 24/7 support desk. Cloud based so accessible to client, bookkeeper and accountant. Other providers of cloud packages may be more suitable for some clients.
*Moneysoft Payroll Manager	Payroll and CIS	Simple and cheap. Particularly suitable for a payroll bureau function with 12 months of identical salaries etc. PC based but only one person uses it (usually).	We prefer this for a payroll bureau. For clients running their own payroll then Xero payroll is more appropriate.
Signable	Online signatures	Simple, cheap and online. UK-based company so same data protection requirements.	Some workflow systems integrate with different software, otherwise Signable would always be our choice.
Hosted Accountants	Online storage and processing	Hosted desktop for PC-based software and data. Allows you to log into your desktop software from anywhere including your phone. Experienced in hosting common accountants' software.	They went through some growing pains at one point but seem back on form now.
Microsoft Office	Office suite – word processor, spreadsheet, presentations, emails, etc.	In common use so integrates with everything and easy to find support.	Move to Office 365 once everything else is cloud based.

Software	Function	Main details	Latest developments
Spotlight Reporting	Management accounts	From simple dash-boards to reports and forecasts.	Pricing structure has changed and is not so cheap when starting up. Also look at Futrli and Fathom.
*Receipt Bank, Expensify, Trip-catcher, DEAR, Vend, Harvest, Stripe, Workflow Max	Other bookkeeping add-ons to Xero, Quickbooks Online (QBO) and other software	All good	There are hundreds of Xero and QBO add-ons to increase the functionality of the core software.
Mailchimp	E-news	Simple and free. One-way integration with Logical Office	Still my favourite although you'll either love or hate the monkey.
Chaser.io	Debt collection	Automatic chasing emails from Xero. Offers more functionality than Xero's own invoice reminders.	
2020 Innova-tion's Tax Tips and Tools	Ad hoc calculations	Spreadsheets to help you calculate: gross/net pay, com-pany car benefits, buy or lease a car, saving on incorpora-tion, comparison of profit extraction methods, etc.	Just pay for the annual update rather than keep updating your own spreadsheets.

* We did not actively look for improvements to this software as it did everything that we wanted.

As you can see from this, even in a highly automated business like ours, there were still plenty of improvements to be made.

Cost versus time saved

Software is of vital importance in the growth of your business. Although you can start off producing accounts and tax calculations on Excel and submitting returns via the HMRC/Companies House free software this is the least efficient method of working.

Bookkeeping done on Excel will require additional work for making tax digital (MTD) as HMRC do not provide software. While spreadsheets are, in theory, acceptable these will still be required to link into the HMRC MTD application programming interface (API).

Initially it is possible to keep a record of client standing data in a spreadsheet and track your work in progress versus deadlines on a spreadsheet or whiteboard. With a manual system like this it is worth also having a page of key numbers and so on, on the front of each client file.

Even when first starting out these skeletal systems will leave you entirely dependent on your own knowledge, with little in the way of the built-in checks which are available in most software.

With a growing business, my gains from each piece of software were also growing.

PC/network versus cloud

No matter how you start out initially, when you take on your first member of staff you will need to consider networks and servers. Servers are expensive to purchase and you will require a second one as a failover. Consider whether you have the ability and inclination to support a server.

I had spent some time at National Grid looking after disaster recovery for the accounts department. We were able to set up desks, software and hardware to get 12 of the 100 accounts staff up and running in a bunker just a couple of hours after we triggered the recovery process. It means that I am very conscious of the high standards that can be achieved by IT professionals with dedicated resources compared to an enthusiastic amateur like me, so I chose to have a hosted desktop where suitable cloud systems were not yet available. This meant that our only vulnerability was our Internet connection and there were plenty of alternative places to go to use the Internet if necessary. Laptops were used as dumb terminals so could be replaced in a matter of hours.

A hosted desktop gives many of the benefits of cloud where suitable software is not available. You can log in from office, home, tablet or phone, although the latter may be challenging with the smaller screen.

The hosting providers take care of all backups and any software upgrades.

Integrated solution or best of breed

When looking for more software I weighed up the benefits and drawbacks of an integrated solution, where data only had to be entered once, versus best of breed, which was just so much better but required duplicate entries.

Integrated

- ▶ Time savings in only maintaining one set of standing data
- ▶ May mean a compromise on individual applications

Best of breed

- ▶ The best solution for you in each application
- ▶ Cheaper

A best of breed route may suit you if the business is not complex and you do not have much change in standing data. The quoted estimates of time saved often appear ridiculous for small businesses but there is definitely some benefit in this area. If I were to make this decision again I would be more inclined towards the integrated approach as my favoured software now has an element of practice management and integration, and a business that has been around for longer often has to change client standing data.

Security

Backups are essential. Initially I was backing up to an external hard drive at the end of each day until a certain small boy, who loved to climb, managed to knock my laptop off my desk on the same day as my external hard drive stopped working (and looked suspiciously as though it had taken a knock too). In spite of my belt and braces I lost a day's work. After this I subscribed to an online backup service which was set to back up everything at 3 pm while I did the school run.

Once we had moved to a hosted desktop they took over the backups.

Xero

Xero deserves a special mention as it revolutionised our business.

I wanted a cloud solution as I definitely liked the idea of interacting with the client regularly and remotely. My disaster recovery experience (these days it's called business continuity, which has a much more positive ring to it) also played a part in wanting client data more secure than I could make it.

We had had a client come to us on Xero a few years earlier and, although I'd liked the software, I was a little concerned that Xero was too new and might not be around in the future. Whenever I go to a conference where I am referred to as an 'early adopter' I still laugh, remembering my initial cynicism.

I examined all sorts of cloud-based packages and was still dithering about which one to choose when Sage launched Sage One. I decided to go for this as I thought that the Sage name would make it easy to convince clients to move over as they had confidence in the brand. We had moved five clients on to the software when I realised that not only was the Sage One software nothing like the Sage Line 50 that clients were used to but that it wasn't anywhere near as good as some of the alternatives at the time. (Sage One has since improved immensely.)

Once I realised my mistake I started the search again. Now that Xero is clearly taking over from Sage as market leader I'm so glad that I reviewed my decision. It is often hard to admit your mistakes even to yourself but it is an essential to moving your business forwards. If you've taken a wrong turn then you need to backtrack or find an alternative route.

Xero still has the best bank feed facility and it continues to hold the bank statement data separately from the bank account data so deleting anything on the accounts side does not also delete it from the statement, thus negating any previous bank reconciliations (one of the things it still does better than Quickbooks Online). We also came across Receipt Bank, which enables clients to submit photos of their receipts or to forward electronic ones. These receipts can then be imported directly into Xero. For both systems it is possible to set bank and supplier rules to automatically code regular transactions. Setting up these rules takes an equivalent amount of time to a standard bank reconciliation in the first month but the second month is around 50 per cent faster and subsequent months are faster still as keying errors are eliminated.

Although we had to pay for all software used in-house (we increased new fees to include it) the time saving was immense and we were able to offer fixed-fee bookkeeping for small clients at a reasonable rate. It also coincided with a bookkeeper friend selling her business.

The nature of our business was changed by this software. The benefits of carrying out monthly bookkeeping for clients in-house are enormous:

- ▶ The data is correctly accounted for
- ▶ The data is up to date and the bank is regularly reconciled
- ▶ Regular contact with the client improves the quality of the relationship
- ▶ Regular contact with the client and their data sometimes leads to spotting opportunities for additional work (but not as often as the accounting gurus and thought leaders would lead us to believe)
- ▶ With good quality data available promptly, the year-end accounts production process is much slicker so there is a time/money saving to the accountant
- ▶ The practice and our clients were well positioned for whatever MTD brings

With data input all but eliminated we were able to focus on services, which added real value to clients:

▶ Useful quarterly reports templates for bookkeeping clients showing a few key figures including a rough tax calculation as well as profit available for dividends so that we didn't have the year-end problem of overdrawn directors' loan accounts.

▶ It only took a few additional reconciliations and journals to produce a management accounts pack from the standard Xero templates and Spotlight Reporting software.

▶ It was viable to offer a free trial of management accounts reports for those clients we felt could benefit from it.

▶ Once we were providing regular management information we were able to add on all sorts of advisory and coaching services.

Xero software also acts as the finance hub to a vast array of business add-ons. We developed the business to integrate these to benefit our clients. Other common add-ons were:

▶ Receipt Bank for all but the smallest clients (in our testing, 16 purchase invoices or expense receipts per month covered the minimum fee)

▶ Chaser for automatic debt collection

▶ Harvest and Workflow Max for project management and time recording

▶ Tripcatcher for tracking mileage (bicycle as well as car)

▶ DEAR for inventory

▶ Stripe or Go Cardless for payments

Although I wasn't initially aware of it when choosing Xero I have since become a great fan because of their collaborative approach. They partner with accountants to provide free training so that we can make the most of their software. As we make their software look good it also makes us look competent when demonstrating or discussing it with clients. This win–win approach to business is one which I very much adopt myself. Quickbooks Online also take this approach. Xero provide access to their API for app developers to work on additional features, which also enhance our reputation as business advisers and not just number crunchers.

There is a lot of work to be done integrating Xero and QBO with various add-ons. This means that the accountant's role is becoming much more technical. While it is worth having skills in-house for common and simple integrations, there are plenty of specialist cloud integrators starting up.

As you can tell, the technology was key to our business growth and easily allowed us to differentiate ourselves with forward thinking clients.

Speed of change

I have also noticed a trend for cloud software companies to release software in a quite basic form and then to continue to develop it post-release. This means that you do not have to wait or pay for the next release as the increased functionality is available to you as soon as it is ready.

I am quite happy to work with such rapidly evolving software but I would suggest that, when you first take on a new piece of software, you double-check what functionality is available today and what is still in development. If functionality is being described then it is probably due out in 6–12 months but you need to know the timescales in order to plan your use of the software.

If you are looking into software for clients to use, or if you are less comfortable with software yourself, then you may need to wait until the functionality that you want/need is actually available. Don't wait too long as, in this rapidly changing market, there will always be something new around the corner and your competitors may well overtake you.

Summary

When choosing your software:

- ▶ Think of it as an investment rather than a benefit.
- ▶ Any time savings due to automation will be increased as your business grows.
- ▶ Decide whether you want an integrated approach or best of breed.
- ▶ Invest in training and setting up your software properly to get the most out of it.
- ▶ Consider what support and training you and your clients will get from the software company.
- ▶ Security is vital and the professionals can do it best.

Chapter 9
Marketing your business

Most accountants have little or no exposure to marketing before starting up.

I had had limited knowledge of this black art, with a single module as part of my chemistry and management degree and, later, working alongside some great strategic and creative marketers in larger businesses. I was fortunate that one of my management accounting roles required some work with the marketing department on their return on investments (ROIs) and the marketing director took me under his wing and taught me a great deal about strategic marketing just because I expressed an interest.

When you start a business in a new part of the country with no personal or business contacts or after a career break, then marketing is essential to your survival. There's nothing like a challenge.

Pros of marketing

- Some sort of marketing (in the broadest sense) is essential to generating new clients
- Allows you to project the best image of who you are and the clients you want

Cons of marketing

- Cost and time
- Difficult to measure what activities are successful
- Most accountants don't know where to start

Issues to consider

- What sort of clients do you want?
- What sort of services can you deliver?
- How soon do you need new clients?
- How much can you spend to accelerate the process?
- How much time do you have?

Simple accounting ideas and material

2020 Innovation, a group of accountancy advisers, were one of the leaders in marketing (amongst other things) for accountants, and definitely innovative. They still provide great value to those who have not run their own practice before. Their ideas often seem very American and may need to be diluted for the UK market but there is so much great material each month that you can pick and choose what you think would work to attract your ideal clients.

Client avatar

The start of good marketing is to define your ideal client and create an avatar. When you first start up and have a scattergun approach this is much easier said than done. My initial aspiration was tied into my personal motivation for my business, so I was looking for prospective clients who were nice people, understood the need to pay for a professional service and that were also capable of paying for this expertise.

Over the years you can refine this avatar as your business grows. At the point I sold my business we were only taking on clients who were serious about their business, and had been around for a few years. They still had to be nice people and we ruled out anyone under the VAT limit, where we didn't think that our advice services were cost-effective, as well as most start-ups unless they had high-growth plans and would take on a full advice package. We even put our starting prices onto our website to reduce the number of unsuitable enquiries.

Types of marketing

There are two main types of marketing: push, where you approach the prospects directly, and pull, where you do things to attract clients. While you need a mixture of both I believe that good pull marketing attracts better clients and commands higher fees.

Examples of push marketing where you actively approach prospects are: advertising and sponsorship, mailshots, e-shots and telephone calls.

Examples of pull marketing are: speaking and writing to demonstrate your expertise as the equivalent of a shop window, networking (both online and offline), signage, website and public relations (PR).

Marketing is often likened to dating, with the process moving from initial awareness to marriage.

It is hard to measure return on marketing as people will usually only tell you the final thing which influenced their decision to contact you, but there is definitely an element of just being around and known for long enough for people to approach you.

I found that a good mailshot would generate 2 per cent leads immediately but of low-level clients.

Our signage and my articles in local publications generated a high number of enquiries but only about half of them were good quality. If you are well known people will come to you because they know you. One of our filters when deciding whether a prospect was right for us was to weed out enquiries which started with 'How much?' as I found that these people were too focused on price rather than value. Another filter was to ask why they were looking at changing their accountant and we were always wary of those who wished to leave other reputable accountants. Just because these enquiries were not suitable for us didn't mean that we couldn't help and we tried to refer them to other local accountants. This helped the client and also generated an element of goodwill.

Networking is a very slow process and takes about 6–12 months to generate leads, although I have been fortunate to pick up a good client the first time I visited a new networking group. See Chapter 4, 'Attending networking events and business shows'.

Speaking/hosting events is the best opportunity to demonstrate exactly what you are about. This has been the source of our best clients but it takes around three years from initial contact to bring them on board. See Chapter 15, 'Speaking at and organising events'.

PR is more effective if you use an expert. Do be aware that you cannot control what is actually written in the press. When I sold my business, one of the local publications used a headline that the Nailsea office was to close, despite the press release making clear that the buyer would retain both offices. Fortunately I spotted the online version and got this corrected. On the other hand another publication used the headline, 'Hundreds [of businesses] to benefit' based on the same press release.

Depending on the type of business that you wish to have, I would recommend some quick wins like mail shots alongside some longer term networking. Once you have enough contacts you can invite then you can begin to develop your own speaking/hosting events.

Steady state marketing

It is important that you do some marketing throughout the year. If you are too busy with the current set of leads to generate the next set then there will be no next set.

The way to do this is to have a marketing plan. You can generate content during quiet periods which can be drip fed through busier times or even delegated to a marketing assistant.

If you attend a networking event but are too busy to follow up immediately (e.g. during December or January) then please at least get an appointment in your diary even if it is a while off.

CRM

A good CRM system is vital to your marketing. See Chapter 8, 'Choosing your software'.

Add on all new contacts who have consented to marketing with a note of how you met them. Update this each time you have another contact with them so that you can see what has the most impact. Adding a little background information is also useful. If you have a poor memory then names of children, favourite football teams and so on are helpful, and if you know how they take their tea or coffee then this can demonstrate that you are interested in them.

Existing clients

Don't forget about your existing clients. These deserve your highest standards of TLC so that they stay with you and are willing to refer new clients to you.

As you have a note of birthdays and so on for tax purposes, it is a nice gesture to send a handwritten card.

New clients

There is a particular welcome window for new clients and I think that accountancy has one of the longest of the professions. This is the period of time it takes for clients to begin to feel loyal. I would estimate that clients need their main handholding for the first two months while all formalities are being completed but this is primarily an admin function. The full welcome window is up until the first piece of work has been submitted, that is, their accounts/returns are all safely put to bed.

Many clients complain that accountants and solicitors do not keep them informed of progress. This is probably because we are, ourselves, fully aware of the timescales of carrying out certain work and dealing with HMRC. It is therefore helpful to give new clients an idea of timescales and a contact name of who will be carrying out the work.

Client of the month

A client of the month competition is a good way to thank your favourite clients, give them a bit of publicity, demonstrate good client behaviour to other clients and generate marketing testimonials. We chose from those who were best aligned with our client avatar and therefore easiest to deal with. We sent them a handwritten thank you card along with some cakes (branded, of course) as well as promoting their business in our monthly e-news. We took the opportunity to say why they were good clients, for example responding to queries promptly, in order to encourage this in others. We also asked them for a quote about how they found our services, which we could use in our e-news and other marketing literature.

Other sources

'Half the money I spend on advertising is wasted; the trouble is I don't know which half.' - John Wanamaker

The key to getting the most out of your marketing money is to have a good strategy. I initially devised mine from the 2020 Innovation ideas and other marketing resources until I discovered *Watertight Marketing*™ (2013) by Bryony Thomas. This book clarified a true marketing process for me.

Where to find help

▶ Watertight Marketing™. Start with buying the book and register this on their website for free updates in order to understand the basics and decide your strategy. The Masterplan programme will help you further but is best carried out with a marketing administrator or similar resource if you do not have the time to do this yourself. I found this an excellent methodology for identifying and setting up the systems required to improve all steps of the considered, thoughtful path to becoming a client of a professional service firm.

▶ 2020 Innovation. Provide plenty of ideas and material and can even carry out some of the work for you. They also provide CPD and other training.

Summary

▶ Decide on your ideal client.
▶ Find out where these ideal clients hang out.
▶ Introduce yourself to them.
▶ Create a simple pathway to get them from the first introduction to their second year.
▶ Spending more will accelerate the process.
▶ Monitor what works best.

Chapter 10

Running training courses

As part of trying to improve our processes we identified that the quality of bookkeeping provided by clients was often of poor quality. They, of course, thought that it was adequate and that it was our job to turn it into a set of accounts. Initially we tried giving them a fairly standard spreadsheet with instructions and then we realised that some of them actually needed training on how to complete the spreadsheet.

This is how we came up with the idea of running simple bookkeeping workshops.

Benefits of running training workshops:

- Better quality information received at year end
- Closer relationship with clients as this provides an opportunity to get to know each other
- Opportunity to market to non-clients who have paid to attend
- Advertising these workshops showed us as proactive accountants
- Advertising our workshops also advertised us as Xero accountants
- Leads to enquiries for bespoke training which can lead to new accounts clients

Cost of running workshops:

- Two people for two hours
- Promotional goods provided
- Refreshments
- Offset by payments from non-clients

How to go about it

Decide your own frequency depending on client requirements and having enough people to make it worthwhile to run the event. We had sufficient interest to run a two-hour evening workshop for up to six people every two to three months. We showed them how to use the spreadsheet and answered some simple questions. It is easy to tag ten minutes onto the end to cover the flat rate VAT scheme.

Consider opening up the training to non-clients. Our workshop was provided free of charge to all clients and there was a charge of £30 to others. It is more efficient to train small numbers of clients together as they often have the same basic questions, but a maximum group size of six makes it simple to tailor the workshop a little to suit their individual needs. Clients will also share nice things about you to the non-clients so it can be very profitable as a marketing exercise.

Consider having two members of staff at each event so that there is no issue with lone working and the second person can arrange refreshments on arrival and halfway through, as well as assisting any slower members to keep up.

Provide everybody with a file, with your logo on it of course, containing a few basic notes and the worked examples that you have covered during the evening. We also gave them a branded pen, pad and a cheap calculator (I couldn't afford to brand this) along with details of our next events.

Having better trained clients will benefit you at year end as you will have better information to work with. You will also establish a closer relationship so that clients are happy to ring you with any bookkeeping queries. This means that matters are resolved straight away and not left until the year end. It also means that the bookkeeping is more likely to be right first time.

Advertising the workshops on social media will made you look like proactive accountants, actively trying to help your clients rather than just saying the words. We used Eventbrite to take bookings and collect any payments. There are other platforms available but this is fairly easy to use and there is no charge for the free places, only the paying ones.

When we discovered Xero with all the online training videos we thought that the need for these courses was past, but we soon found that some clients preferred to attend a face-to-face session. We made no secret of the fact that training was available free of charge online as we advertised the new Xero bookkeeping workshops to clients and non-clients. The benefit was that attendees could ask questions in real time with examples from their own accounts where appropriate.

Although we advertised the same topics on each workshop it was usually possible to tweak them on the night to accommodate all attendees.

In promoting the beginners' workshops we also had enquiries from existing Xero users who wanted further training and some tips on how to do things better or faster. We began to offer this on an hourly basis, charging slightly more for one of our bookkeepers to travel to their premises. With a single exception, every non-client who approached us for this one-to-one training later came on board as an accounts client. This is another example of them paying for us to build a relationship and gently market to them.

Checklist for running training

- ▶ Beforehand:
  - ▷ Set up the event on Eventbrite and website
  - ▷ Promote through social media and monthly e-news
  - ▷ Invite all new clients at your initial meeting and follow up any other interested parties
- ▶ On the night:
  - ▷ Produce notes and files for each attendee
  - ▷ Set up a large screen for demonstrations
  - ▷ Prepare a goody bag of promotional items for attendees to carry their files and so on home afterwards
  - ▷ Prepare refreshments including biscuits and, for us, our signature jelly beans
  - ▷ Arrange meeting room including pop-up banner

Who can help?

Xero 101 on XeroTV has some good basic training videos and there is a demo company set up within Xero itself. You can base your training on this. We considered showing the video then talking people through a hands-on example but found that complete customisation was more suitable.

For other software you may need to create your own training from scratch but the Xero webinars will give you some examples of what to include.

Summary

Running in-house training events is one of those lovely opportunities for everybody to win:

- ▶ Clients receive training.
- ▶ You receive better quality bookkeeping so year-end work will be faster.
- ▶ You get to know your clients better.
- ▶ There is a little bit of passive marketing to the non-clients present.
- ▶ Advertising the events increases your profile in the business community.

Chapter 11
Networking through
social media

Social media can help your small business to punch above your weight. This is one area where I truly believe that small firms can do better than our larger competitors. Our small town accountancy business used Twitter and other social media to become 20th and 27th in the Economia 50 list of top financial influencers in different years and led to me being asked to speak on the subject at Accountex in 2018.

Pros of social media

- ▶ Extends your influence beyond what is possible in person
- ▶ Can be fitted around your working day
- ▶ Zero cash outlay is required
- ▶ It's a great way for introverts to network
- ▶ It's about more than just marketing

Cons of social media

- ▶ Takes a lot of time (hours spent and elapsed time) to achieve real results
- ▶ Privacy, trolling and the not nice side of human beings

Issues to consider

- ▶ What do you want to achieve from your use of social media?
- ▶ Where do your prospective clients hang out?
- ▶ Who will look after your social media accounts? In-house or outsourced?
- ▶ How much time do you have?
- ▶ Which channel(s) will you use?

Using social media because somebody says you should isn't a good enough reason. Think of what you want to achieve so that you make best use of your online time.

We used social media to connect with:

- ▶ Potential clients. To get to know them and let them know that we existed.
- ▶ Current clients. As an informal way of keeping in touch with them.

- Introducers. To let them know what we were doing and to support them where we could.
- Suppliers. To see what they were up to and new services/products they could offer us, even if not right now.
- Other good accountants. To collaborate and share best practice.
- Interesting people. Because life is too short not to.

Which platform is best?

In an ideal world you would have a decent representation on all channels. In reality you will probably have one primary channel, one secondary and an almost dormant account on a few others.

- LinkedIn is for business and this suited us well as we helped businesses to grow.
- Facebook is more for consumers and was of limited use for us as we dealt exclusively with businesses and not with private individuals.
- Twitter is a mixture of business and individuals and this is where I spent most time. Its informal but brief style suits me very well. It is an excellent platform to demonstrate the human side of your professional business.
- Instagram is predominantly visual and you may find artistic clients here, or those with a visual product.
- Snapchat is considered to be good for marketing amongst younger prospective clients and employees if you make use of the stories.

Where to start

Create the best first impression possible. The default egg or silhouette avatar does not encourage anyone to interact with you and logos are also a poor choice as 'people buy from people'. Professionally taken head shots are surprisingly cheap and the right lighting can be flattering while still keeping you recognisable.

Use the same photo across all your social media so that people can follow you across platforms.

Keep your photograph current. I once arranged to talk to a potential supplier whom I hadn't met before. She was blonde in her photograph; however, she turned out to be brunette in real life (IRL); fortunately she recognised me from my own head shot and we began a good business relationship.

Ensure that your key contact information is in your profile.

Your profile is the equivalent of your formal introduction so be clear what you do but keep it brief. On Twitter it is appropriate to include hobbies as well as business facts.

What to post

This varies with each channel. The rule of thumb that I was given when I first set out on Twitter was that your updates should be one third social, one third general business and one third specifically about your business. Any of you who follow me on Twitter or connect with me on LinkedIn will see that I have evolved to suit my own style, but I still believe that this mix is a good guide. Too much social stuff and you don't get your message across; too much about your business and people will switch off.

LinkedIn has less social chat and Facebook has much more so choose your main platform to suit your style.

Social chat is about your hobbies, for example golf and family, that will encourage people to interact with you on a human level.

General business can be sharing other people's content which relates to your own industry or which may be of interest to your followers. It may be general blogs that you have created yourself.

Your own business posts can be invitations to events, links to your videos, updates on what you've been doing, successes of your trainees in exams and so on. Trainees are particularly good, their success reflects well on you and the 'selfie generation' are quite comfortable for you to post a smiling photo of them on social media. Don't post photographs without their agreement.

Every platform has its own language so posting the same update across several media without changing it just looks as though you can't be bothered.

Twitter has just 280 characters (it was previously 140, which was more of an intellectual challenge) to get your message across so the style is fairly informal and proper grammar sometimes slips to accommodate this, but I suggest that you don't lapse all the way into text speak if you are promoting a business.

Facebook has a very informal style and pictures work well, although perhaps not the ones of that drunken night in Ibiza.

LinkedIn is more for professionals and this is the language to adopt. Not full-blown manager-speak as that is just nonsense but the sort of language that you use with your business clients.

Avoid politics and religion unless you feel strongly enough for your business to succeed or fail due to your beliefs. While I would always aim not to offend anyone, my view was that if they were offended by something that I posted then they probably weren't suitable clients for us anyway.

Time

While social media may appear to be free marketing it can be very heavy on your time so this is something to factor into your planning.

There are ways to reduce the amount of time spent by scheduling updates with something like a Hootsuite dashboard. You can use Hootsuite free of charge but the professional version is only around US$99 a year and allows you to bulk upload your posts to multiple platforms.

Make a monthly plan of the business updates that you want to share amongst your less formal real-time posts. I schedule three a day on Twitter, and one a day on each of LinkedIn and Facebook, which move at a slower pace. In line with the different platform styles I do not put identical posts on all channels but rewrite each one.

If you use the free version you have to cut and paste these into Hootsuite manually. However, the professional version allows you to upload from a spreadsheet and even shortens links, which is important if you use Twitter with its limit of 280 characters, and can make your posts quick and easy to read.

That's the official stuff done relatively quickly.

Then log in at times which suit you.

At 7 am, while I drink my first cup of tea, I catch up on what has been going on, comment on updates which interest me and share anything that I think may be of interest to a selection of my followers. This hour is a dead time when I can't do any other business so it works well for me.

I also log in around 5 pm while I'm cooking dinner for my kids and supervising their homework at the kitchen table. It's another time when I can't be doing other business.

Depending how busy my day is, I may log in during the day and I also receive notifications either direct from the app or via email when somebody interacts with me.

If you are going to use social media you need to respond to people within a reasonable space of time. One client used a so-called social media expert to tweet for them. Twice she took two weeks to respond to one of my tweets. It was a poor representation of a business which is very customer focused and they have since stopped using this expert. On Twitter you need to log in most days.

On any medium you must be available whenever you are running a campaign. If you post something people will respond. I know several people who schedule their posts for a month as I do but only respond once a week. This has meant that they've missed the opportunity of referrals that I have made to them and probably others too.

Outsourcing your social media

There are digital agencies who will look after your social media for you, but I have always had difficulty working out who the good ones are.

They need to really understand your business, both the brand and the personality. Digital Mums are quite good at this for small businesses but their basic package is often not enough. You may well need to post additional messages or to respond to queries, so be clear about who will do what.

Your agency needs to be responsive to comments and enquiries, or perhaps you could look after this part of it in-house. One client used an agency that posted good interactive content but twice took over a week to respond to my tweets. This was not representative of how the company looked after their customers so they soon stopped using the agency.

Some firms delegate their social media to a junior who is comfortable with the technology, but it is still important for them to understand your brand and your objectives. It is best to agree a framework and tone of voice for what and how they post, but they should still refer anything tricky to you before responding impulsively and, possibly, unprofessionally.

This requirement for a consistent tone of voice is the main reason why using social media makes it so easy for small firms to make a big impact compared to the more regulated postings of large, faceless organisations. An exception to this is Xero who have a small team around the world chatting online in-between the more formal information posts.

So how should you approach social media?

Think of it as an extension of real-life networking.

As you enter the room you and others say hello, ask how each other are, how business is going and then start a conversation and perhaps introduce a few other people who can help.

You don't walk into a room with a paper bag over your head or a business card covering your smile. In my case I often have strangers introducing themselves to me at the supermarket, dance classes or even on the bus.

When you enter the room do you stand in the corner or do you say 'hello' when somebody speaks to you? While it is easy to lurk on social media please do interact with people. On social media you have an opportunity to post a short biography about yourself. Read other people's and you can often find a question to ask them about themselves.

In real life you wouldn't thrust your business card or an advert at people until you've at least said 'hello'. If people have no idea who you are or whether they even like you, let alone trust you to do something for their business, then you need to address this before posting adverts. Even when that time comes it is more subtle to include links to case studies.

I know a cleaning company who are very committed to training their staff well. Yes, they have a brochure and a website that say that but they also post photos of their training evenings. I remember the photographs because they had some very nice looking cakes. Visual images work well.

One business posted a picture of a café where they were holding their board meeting and pointed out that you don't need a permanent office. This seemed really great and I loved the view. Sometimes I work from home or from a local gastropub with fabulous views. When the same business had posted similar photos several times in one week it started to look as though they weren't actually serious about their business. Don't post too many photos of cake – unless you are a baker, of course.

Who should you connect with on social media?

Use each platform differently as there is a slightly different audience or they have a different purpose.

On LinkedIn I connect with people whom I have met or developed a relationship with through online interaction.

On Facebook I am more cautious as this is linked to my personal account with information about my family and children.

On Twitter I connect with anybody who interests me, local Bristol businesses, local competitors, accountants elsewhere whom I respect and other business people I like and respect. I can't remember how I first met the cleaning company I mentioned but they are happy with their accountant so are neither a client nor a potential client. Similarly I'm happy with my cleaning company. If that ever changes we'll be in touch but, in the meantime, we share good and bad things about our businesses and they make me smile.

LinkedIn

LinkedIn is used in a different way and interaction is much slower and more formal than Twitter or Facebook.

I would expect to see weekly updates on LinkedIn of such things as links to blog posts or other informative articles. There is less individual interaction and less social posting.

Join groups of people likely to use your services. As well as being members of various national accountancy and business groups as a means of gathering information, you could join one of the local business groups and become active on their forums. Post a well phrased but leading question to encourage people to interact with you. A few days later post follow-up questions and don't forget to interact with those who respond. Be very careful not to tip the balance over into selling. This is still all about relationships.

Developing relationships in real life

As well as connecting with people whom I have met personally, I like to meet up with people whom I interact with regularly online. Please observe all the usual safety rules that you would teach your kids. Meet in a public place; a business networking event is good but otherwise a café or their office or yours, unless your office is your home.

Do a little more research on the person before you meet and make sure that somebody knows where you are going.

It is very odd to meet somebody whom you have known online for a couple of years, perhaps interacting with them most days. You feel as though you know a lot about them, but actually most of what you know is what they have told you about themselves, so do beware. If I meet somebody for the first time in person I expect to shake their hand, but if I meet somebody for the first time after a two-year online relationship it wouldn't be unusual to greet them with an air kiss in the method of reunited friends. You may or may not be comfortable with this, but please be wary.

Safety online

Make a decision about your privacy. I chose not to post recognisable photographs of my kids nor their names or ages. My home was initially my registered office address and I was easy to find.

I tried using a separate Facebook account with fairly open settings but I eventually deleted it due to some sexually explicit comments that were posted. This is partly why I keep fairly close privacy settings on my personal account. Privacy settings are constantly changing so do keep on top of them. Both Twitter and Facebook seem to attract trolls and even LinkedIn has its own oddities. Trolls are people who sit behind the safety of their keyboards and seem to have nothing better to do than post insults online.

The best rule is not to feed the trolls. If their comments fall within certain criteria of the social media platform you can report them. On Twitter you can block them. The main thing to remember is *do not feed the trolls*. Like any bully they will usually go away if you ignore them.

Beware of the personal information that you post online. Consider what precautions you would tell your children to take. If I go away on holiday I do not talk about it until afterwards as I don't want strangers to know that my home will be empty. Similarly if I happen to be in the office on my own.

While most people online are as lovely as they are in real life do take these basic precautions.

Summary

▶ Know why you are using social media.
▶ Decide which platforms will suit your purpose and style best.
▶ Use a professionally taken photograph across all platforms.
▶ Share a mixture of content: social, general business and your business.
▶ Photographs and short videos work well.
▶ Interact with people.
▶ Stay safe online.

Chapter 12

Moving into premises

Many sole practitioners work from home and never want or need to move to external premises. One colleague told me how, for his first client meeting, he put some empty files on top of the piano and moved a phone onto the dining table even though it wasn't connected to anything.

Options to consider:

- ▶ Working from home
- ▶ Serviced offices
- ▶ Your own premises

Working from home

It takes self-discipline to work from home so this is not for everyone, although it may be the only real choice if you have young children and limited childcare. If you can have a dedicated office within the home this will limit interruptions and keep client information confidential. Unless you keep the door locked it does not stop the rest of the family from borrowing your stapler and so on and failing to return it.

If you're working from home the biggest decision is whether you will see clients at home or will you always visit their premises or meet in coffee shops or elsewhere. If you work alone there are risks to seeing people in unknown places or to inviting them into your home.

We deliberately bought a former post office with space for a professional looking office at the front. With a large shop window any visitors were clearly visible from the road and a peep hole and a step gave me the advantage on whether I even wanted to admit callers. The door was kept locked as a default.

Ensure that there are no restrictions on the use of the premises. Read your house deeds properly as many new estates do not allow their freeholders to run a business from home. This is to avoid huge volumes of commercial traffic on a residential street. You will also need to consider whether it is appropriate to have any sort of signage. A small plaque is useful to confirm that visitors are in the right place.

As a former post office some of our home's original signage is still visible, but it was unclear whether the original business use had ever officially become residential. In order to put up a sign, I decided to play it safe and choose between either have planning permission to run a business from our premises or to apply for planning permission to put up an advertising board. I opted for the former. There are planning regulations on the size and nature of signage. The main sign was put up while our removals van was unloading and my parents also gave me a traditional brass plaque to put outside by the main door, something that I'd dreamed of when I first started training even if it isn't so relevant these days.

Remember to notify your insurance company that your home is used for business purposes, although there will probably be no increase in costs until you exceed a certain number of visitors/staff per week.

Your local council may also be interested in charging business rates. We got agreement from the ratings valuation inspector that the front office was mixed use as it also served as my home office. When the back office was no longer able to double up as a guest room this had to be classed as business premises, but it fell below the small business limit so there was nothing to pay. Do be proactive in sorting out your rates because the small business rate relief cannot be backdated. On the other hand we had lost Principal Private Residence Relief (PPR) on this part of our home so there would potentially be capital gains tax to pay on the eventual sale of the house.

You can claim a proportion of your domestic costs as a business expense. For a sole trader this is a straight apportionment but, as a limited company, the director charges the company rent and then claims the costs against their personal rental income.

If you are desperate to stay working from home you could consider storing your archiving and marketing materials at another location.

Serviced offices

These are great for one or more people. As an accountant you probably need a private office rather than a shared one because of confidentiality issues. Your rent and telephone/Internet charges will cover all costs including a shared reception so it is easy to budget. You may have refreshments and meeting rooms included or these will be available to hire.

Serviced offices are ideal for a growing business as you only pay for the space that you are using at any particular time and it is usually relatively easy to take on additional space without changing address.

Your own premises

I had been looking at premises for some time just to see what I could get for my money. Then I bought a bookkeeping practice. The additional staff and subcontractors forced us to move out of my home and we decided to go to a local shopping centre just two miles up the road in the nearest town.

In choosing new premises you need to consider:

▶ the size of premises including and excluding any shared facilities such as toilets and kitchens

▶ a separate meeting room or office for seeing clients

▶ having a room large enough to hold events, which will mean that you could run more of them

▶ having space for good signage visible from the ground floor

▶ the total cost including rent, service charges, rates and insurance plus an allowance for utilities. As a rule of thumb the total cost of premises will be about twice the rent

▶ the location of premises for you and staff

▶ parking and public transport for staff and clients

▶ the length of lease and any break clauses

▶ whether you, as director, have to guarantee the lease thus negating the value of having a limited liability company

▶ whether your business would be better off in a town centre or business park location.

If the premises are in need of a great deal of work you could negotiate a rent free period to offset the cost of some of that work. We managed to get our refurbishment work done before we officially signed the lease thanks to a very amenable landlord's agent. We were taking a risk in getting the work completed before signing the lease but I kept an eye on committed costs as well as the progress of the lease.

It is worth using a solicitor for the lease as they can prove very practical in explaining which clauses you could/should change and which ones the landlord is unlikely to move on and what this would mean to you.

Having third-party premises means that you will have to make more effort to ensure that the premises are manned during normal office hours and possibly make additional arrangements for lone working. We installed a magnetic door lock that could be operated via a handset upstairs and a separate lock on our own office door as other residents shared our toilet facilities. There were a few other users who were given the code for the downstairs door by the landlord.

How to find premises

Tell everybody that you are looking, how much space you need and where. Contact local commercial agents and, if you only want a small office, it may be worth contacting your local residential agents too. There is no single website for commercial property and even the agents' own websites have little information.

The simplest way to find property or agents is to drive around the area you are hoping to move to as agents will usually post boards outside vacant premises. Once you get in touch they may well have other sites available.

Signage

Signage is useful in publicising where you are to prospects and first-time visitors. In order to make the most of the footfall in the shopping centre where we had our new offices, we had the traditional shopfront sign over the ground floor entrance plus a more informative sign/ad on a transparency in the window. The most important sign was a 'wayfinder' that stuck out from the building for people to see from further away. Remember that people are unlikely to be looking directly at your office but will be looking along the road. As our offices had a shared staircase I made a cheeky request to put a modern three-dimensional sign outside our upstairs door and this was granted. It is always worth asking for what you want, politely.

Moving list

Things to arrange when moving offices:

- ▶ Rent and service charges
- ▶ Rates
- ▶ Utilities
- ▶ Phone and broadband
- ▶ Moving servers unless you are cloud based or have a hosted desktop
- ▶ Removals (it is worth getting more than one person along with their van)
- ▶ Additional furniture required (there are some good second-hand office furniture stores)
- ▶ IT infrastructure – cabling or Wi-Fi for staff plus guest Wi-Fi
- ▶ Signage
- ▶ Introducing yourself to neighbours and warning them of the extent of any temporary disruption while you move in

- ▶ Change of address notifications to clients, contacts and HMRC by email and letter if possible
- ▶ Change of address on all marketing material
- ▶ Change of address on letter templates, email footers and so on
- ▶ Mail forwarding
- ▶ Buildings and contents insurance
- ▶ New risk assessments for health and safety
- ▶ Building work and decoration if required
- ▶ Refreshments during relocation (and perhaps a bottle of champagne to christen your new home)
- ▶ Office warming party for clients and contacts
- ▶ TV licence and PRS (Performing Right Society) licences for streaming TV and/or playing music in the office
- ▶ Press release about your new premises
- ▶ Delegate the project management of the move to a competent member of the team if possible

Chapter 13
Controlling your cash flow

Turnover is vanity
Profit is sanity
Cash is king

I can't find who originally said that but it is very true.

Lack of cash is the main reason that small businesses fail but many people still don't prioritise their cash flow.

Ways to improve your cash flow:

- ▶ Increase income (see Chapter 5, 'Setting your prices')
- ▶ Get paid sooner
- ▶ Reduce bad debts
- ▶ Reduce outgoings (see Chapter 6, 'Budgeting and controlling costs')
- ▶ Pay suppliers later

Starting up

When you set up a company you need to pay for certain things, probably immediately as you have no credit rating, or there is a financial penalty for extended payment terms.

Getting paid sooner

Traditionally, even once you have a client signed up you have to wait for their year end, chase the work in, do the work and then invoice before you will receive any cash.

By charging fixed fees you and your client will know, in advance, what the annual fee will be. Most small businesses are happy to spread this cost over 12 months rather than face a large bill, even if it is much later. This means that you and they have more predictable cash flow.

With predictable income you can arrange collections by standing orders. These are free but need to be updated by the client for price increases and one-offs. You could also collect by direct debit, which is under your control but has an associated cost. Our usual terms were monthly payments, with half the annual fee paid before the year end, which sometimes meant a larger initial payment if the client came to us after their year end.

The additional benefits were reduced credit control costs and, as you won't be constantly chasing invoices, a better relationship with clients because there are no surprise bills.

If you are already in business and worried about switching to monthly payments please be reassured that most clients actually prefer to pay this way. If you are still wary then start with new clients only and perhaps a simple circular email offering this method to your existing clients. I estimate that around a third will sign up immediately with a further third signing up when prompted a second or third time. It is then up to you whether you chase the stragglers but your cash flow will have improved from two thirds of your clients.

For clients who did not wish to spread the cost we required full payment up front when we received their books. The practical problem with this was that we had relatively few clients paying annually so it was easy to miss invoicing them and we soon ceased to offer this option.

Even without fixed fees you can ask for payment on account and staged payments. Be careful to specify these stages in your original contract terms and don't leave them to the client to determine. Take care to avoid such stages as 'approval' of work as this is very vague and it may be that the work is never 'approved'.

You are an accountant, not a bank. Your business is not lending money to clients through extended credit terms. Ensure that you get paid as much up front as possible and chase debts as soon as they become overdue. This is also what you should be teaching your clients to do in their own businesses.

Football clubs issue season tickets which are paid for in March for a season that doesn't even start until August let alone finish until the following May, so fans are paying 5–14 months before receipt of 'goods'. And these don't even come with a quality guarantee as most dedicated fans will know. If even football clubs with multimillion pound losses can get their customers/fans paying this far in advance then why can't accountants?

For those unable to pay for the season up front then our local club have negotiated a season ticket loan facility with a third party. The fan pays the additional cost of this and the club receive the cash immediately. You could refer your clients to similar financiers.

How to minimise bad debts or slow payment

Remember that a sale is not a sale until it has been paid.

▶ Check your prospect's credit rating before you try to sell to them. Perhaps they are keen to try a new accountant because they have exhausted their credit facilities elsewhere. If you later find that you've sold to poor credit risks you can end up paying for staff time, software and so on but never receive any payment in return. If you have to wait a long time to receive payment then you need to find a way to pay your own suppliers and your staff salaries in the meantime.

▶ Make sure that your terms and conditions of sale are clear. These should be specified in your engagement letter and on your invoice.

▶ On completion of work you could arrange a courtesy call to check that the client is happy, and that they have received the invoice and approved it for payment. This gives you time to rectify any perceived problems with the service.

▶ If payment is not received on the due date then call straight away. This can be a polite enquiry to ensure that everything is OK. If payment is delayed can they give you an expected date so that you can negotiate your overdraft? Decide whether to continue working with this client.

▶ Seven days later or whenever the payment was promised chase them again, perhaps with a formal letter. You can then start a series of letters leading to legal action if the debt is still unpaid.

▶ If you use Xero then some of this chasing can be automated with invoice reminders. Alternatively Chaser.io connects to both Xero and Quickbooks Online and provides a more sophisticated reminder system.

Paying your suppliers later

Always pay your suppliers on your agreed terms.

You can negotiate longer payment terms or it is often possible to pay some bills, such as insurances, over 12 months for little or no extra cost.

There is a cost of administration when making payments so it may be simpler to make payments on receipt of invoice or on a fixed day each week or month.

How to obtain finance including overdrafts

Having a business plan and management accounts is key to arranging finance. This is how you can explain your business to the bank (or alternative) and how you show that you can afford to pay their interest charges as well as repaying their loan. Not only are the management accounts themselves important as part of obtaining finance, but the fact that they are readily available shows that you are truly in control of your business and understand the financial implications of your business decisions.

Armed with your management accounts and cash flow forecast you should have no problem obtaining finance as banks are still happy to lend in low-risk situations. Banks will lend to support expansion or growth and our clients have received finance for their acquisitions. Banks will not lend to support ongoing losses with no realistic plan for repayment.

You can also look at invoice finance as a short-term or ongoing source of cash. There are various ways of assigning your invoices and costs will vary accordingly.

For bigger projects or for start-ups you may need to look beyond banks. Take a look at Capitalisers.com, a service which is free to accountants to access multiple financiers at once. It's a bit like MoneySuperMarket but for business finance. If you don't need the cash immediately then it is often cheaper to agree finance ahead of time.

Summary

You need cash to pay for many things in your business but you also need cash from the company to pay for many things in your personal life. You need cash to book your holiday, you need cash to buy your child's birthday present and you will, eventually, need cash to live on in retirement.

In order to do this you will need to:

- ▶ Get more money in sooner.
- ▶ Only deal with creditworthy clients unless you receive payment in advance.
- ▶ Consider arranging access to finance for clients.
- ▶ Pay less money out and later.
- ▶ Plan your cash flow requirements in plenty of time.

Chapter 14

Becoming a trusted adviser

Surveys keep telling us that accountants are a business's most trusted adviser and accounting gurus are telling us that compliance is dead so we need to move to a more advisory role in order to add value to clients. But do you have to and how?

Pros of advisory work

- Personally I love this type of work as I like to help improve the numbers and not just record them
- Add value to clients
- Increased fees
- Future-proof your business as more of the compliance work is automated
- Offering good business advice differentiates you from other accountants

Cons of advisory work

- Not all accountants enjoy this type of work
- Compliance work is much simpler
- Advisory work usually means more client interaction which may not suit everybody
- Competing against unqualified advisers makes it hard to differentiate your services
- Not all clients want/need advisory services
- Not all accountants have the business skills to offer business advice

Issues to consider

Many accountants' websites claim to offer business advice but, on closer inspection, they turn out to offer cash flow forecasts and assistance with getting finance from banks or others. To me business advice is much broader than this and includes most of the subjects covered in this book. You may choose to do it yourself or to work with a team of associates and specialists.

Realistically consider your personal skills to decide on the best way to do this, if at all. As my background is in running businesses I found that I could offer an introduction to most of the key areas for a new business owner. I also built a network of experts to refer to for specialist advice. The idea was to have a team that represented all the functions around the boardroom table plus a few more besides. Whether you go down the advisory route or not it is still worth having these sort of contacts.

The full advisory service

In order to provide a suitable service you will need up-to-date financial and business information. This is much easier with modern cloud software and the bookkeeping function can be split between the client, bookkeeper and accountant as appropriate. The accountant can then produce management accounts and forecasts at the agreed frequency.

If you are using Xero or Quickbooks Online there are a number of management accounting and forecasting add-ons that will enable you to produce colourful and meaningful (do sense check!) reports at the touch of a button. Take a look at Spotlight, Futrli, Fathom and Float. You will probably have a preference and most businesses will only use one of these or two at most.

You will also need to know where the client is heading. For a sole business owner their business goals reflect their personal goals and so we used to cover both as part of our strategic planning day. In a company with multiple business owners you will find a range of personal goals and so each business needs to be run to achieve all of these, or it can be made clear that some of them are not possible.

Now you have your destination and also the means of monitoring where you are on the road. Your purpose is to help the business owner to steer towards the destination, making any course corrections along the way.

The knowledge to help with this can come from formal business training, regular reading, practical experience and/or translating ideas from one business to another.

Alternatives

If you decide not to go down the advisory route then there are still things that you can do to differentiate yourself and to improve your relationship with your clients.

Client feedback surveys can be used to discover what clients think you do well and also what improvements or additional services (or introductions) you could provide.

We found that our in-house events, such as Money Matters seminars and Xero training, were a great way to demonstrate our expertise and provide a bit of extra benefit, at a relatively low cost once we had our own meeting room.

Keeping in regular contact allows you to strengthen your relationship as well as to identify any additional client requirements. A simple monthly e-news is a good way to do this. You could also consider sending birthday cards as you hold clients' dates of birth. This prompted several positive comments from clients. Social media and networking events are often seen as a way to generate new leads but they were also a great way to keep in touch with existing clients.

Not everyone wants meetings face to face but it is usually better to offer a meeting before year ends to look forwards rather than afterwards just to sign accounts.

Customer service that wows

Having a consistently high level of service can be achieved through good systems with a helpful human interface. Walk through your client experience and make improvements along the way which are easy to replicate. Make sure that:

- ▶ All your marketing sends a consistent message.
- ▶ Your website is clear and easy to interact with on all devices. Check the speed at which it opens.
- ▶ Your phone is answered consistently and any messages passed on. There are times when you are in the office but deep in concentration. You will need to be clear when you are and aren't available to clients and how your receptionist or answering service will deal with questions at these times.
- ▶ You have response times for returning phone calls and replying to emails. Large organisations might take three to five days to respond to enquiries but they usually set an autoresponder to reply to initial emails so that the client has an expectation. Personally I think small organisations are better able to provide a next day response at the latest. Work out what you can consistently manage and then stick to this or better.
- ▶ You create the right first impression to visitors. Look at your reception area or entrance through clients' eyes. Does it inspire them with confidence in your ability to run a successful business without appearing to waste their fees?
- ▶ Your fees are clear from the beginning. These can be on your website, with your engagement letter and on invoices. Avoid surprises for your client.

- Your paperwork is all in order and particular care taken on entering client names into your system(s). It creates a better impression if the small details are right from the beginning.

- You keep explanations clear and simple. Accountants are often accused of treating knowledge as power. The taxpayer is ultimately responsible for signing their tax return so do explain as much of this as you think they need and anything else that they ask too. Most of our work is simple.

- Use email templates for common purposes as this allows you to be consistent, but do try to personalise them as far as possible.

- Communicate! Clients don't understand the work involved after they've dropped their books to their accountant and why it can sometimes take so long to complete the work. If you haven't ordered a Domino's pizza online before then treat yourself and look at how they visually share the preparation, cooking and delivery of your meal on their website. Another example is the way Uber can show where your taxi is while it is on its way to you. You don't need a fancy application to do this but look at simpler ways to keep your client informed.

Out-of-hours service

Replying to client emails outside office hours might look good at the time but this will soon become the expectation. Consider whether you want to be tied to this once you have a team who only work nine to five. When I first set up my business I offered support up until 9 pm to compensate for the fact that I was not usually available 3–8 pm because of my children. I soon dropped this from our advertising once I had a team.

The same applies to out-of-hours meetings. While you might tweak a 5 pm finish to 6 pm, anyone serious about their business will make time to see their accountant during business hours. If you have a lot of private clients you could offer one late night per month or per week so that you and your team can plan around this and, hopefully, take a morning off to compensate. Asking around other professionals; weekend meetings seem to have a high incidence of no-shows and I had a similar experience so I stopped offering these after the first year.

Who can help?

Both Xero and Quickbooks Online provide a great deal of practice management training to their accountant partners. 2020 Innovation are also very good for this.

There are many generic books on customer service that you can draw on. Most of the extras are just TLC and cost little. They can be as basic as decent coffee and tea or offering to charge mobiles during meetings.

Avoiding pitfalls

Decide the type of services that you want to offer and then look for clients who want these services. If you are keen to help businesses to grow by offering the right advice then it is best to look for prospects with growing businesses and the understanding and ability to pay. If you want to stick to compliance then look at efficiencies in processing but add on a few 'extras' to make you look like better value.

Getting clients who fit your standard offering will allow you to give them the best service as all your resources will be focused on this. We awarded a client of the month both to thank that client but also to highlight the type of clients that we wanted. For example,

X is our client of the month because regular management accounts and forecasting have allowed them to grow Y per cent.

or

A is our client of the month because they always keep their Xero bank reconciliations up to date so that they have up-to-date information to run their business.

Ensure that you charge enough to cover the costs of the service that you have sold. You cannot offer a premium service on a shoestring.

Summary

- ▶ Decide whether you want to provide advisory services.
- ▶ Decide who will provide them: you or trusted colleagues.
- ▶ Ensure that the compliance work is of a suitable standard to provide timely and useful information.
- ▶ If you are not providing advisory services (or even if you are) there are other things that you can do in order to become the first port of call for clients' enquiries.

Chapter 15
Speaking at and organising events

Why?

Retailers have a shop window and customers often have the opportunity to touch and feel their products before customers buy. The equivalent for service clients is to offer some (free) advice and an opportunity to get to know the expert. The difficulty with this is the balance between providing something useful and not giving away your most valuable knowledge.

Workshops and webinars are also a good way to train several people at once making it more profitable for you and cheaper for them.

Pros of running events

▶ Speaking to lots of people in one place

▶ Introduction as an expert

▶ An opportunity for clients and prospects to meet more of the team or to see inside your offices

▶ Have details of all attendees to follow up

▶ A series of events can create a reputation and a differentiator from your competitors

▶ Although many accountants describe themselves as proactive, this is a way to demonstrate that you really are by providing information up front

Cons of running events

▶ Most people would rather appear naked in public than speak to a room full of people

▶ Costs of venue, refreshments and goody bags

▶ Hassle of promoting your own event

Issues to consider

▶ Do you want to host the event yourself?

▶ Will you charge for the event?

▶ Is the event for existing clients or for others?

▶ Is it a technical event or a general business one?

▶ Is it for a particular sector, for example contractors, tech, or food and drink? Or general?

- What time of day will you hold the event?
- Could you run webinars that are cheaper but give less opportunity to interact with your attendees?
- How will you promote the event?
- Where will you hold the event?
- How many will you invite and how many do you expect to attend?
- What refreshments will you provide?
- What will you hand out in goody bags?
- How will you follow up the contacts from the event?

Organising your event

What time of day?

Breakfast, mid-morning, lunchtime, after work or evening all have their pros and cons. We found that after work was best overall although this did make it harder for working mothers and others who bear the brunt of childcare.

Finding venues and charging structures

You will need to estimate how many people you expect to turn up for your event in order to book the appropriate sized room. This needs to be done in plenty of time for you to include the venue on your promotional material. There are often no-shows, especially with free events, and sometimes walk-ins.

We particularly liked a venue that had a variety of room sizes so that, although we booked for one size, they could usually accommodate a change of room at a fairly late stage. They only charged us for the actual room used, even if it was a smaller one than planned.

Charging structures are usually for the room plus extras. You can usually negotiate for projectors and flipcharts to be included. It is worth carrying spare flipchart and whiteboard pens. It is normal to pay extra for refreshments and you will probably be quite surprised how much you will be charged for an urn of hot water and a few packets of biscuits. Most venues need you to confirm numbers a week before the event so you will have to estimate how many you expect to turn up. If you book tea and coffee on arrival this will sometimes do for halfway through too. Again, our favourite venue is the only one that allowed us to confirm final numbers on the day so we only paid for what was used.

If you can afford it I would highly recommend premises with a decent-sized meeting room where you can hold events for up to 20 people without having to pay. Once we had this resource we were able to run seminars and training much more frequently and thus increased our exposure in the business community.

Charging for the event

Free events have higher bookings but lower proportional attendance. This may vary according to the area. When we first started organising events in hired locations in the city centre we had 50 per cent turnout, which is what we had been told to expect for free events. When we moved to our own premises in a town just outside the city we no longer needed to commit to numbers a week ahead of time. We also found that the turnout, outside the main city, was 100 per cent with the exception of the odd person who had the courtesy to contact us beforehand to let us know that they would not be attending

Free events are more attractive to start-ups so you may wish to focus on those who are further along their business journey or can afford to pay more for your valuable services.

A nice move is to make a nominal charge that will be donated to a charity. This will encourage people to book only if they are serious.

Finding speakers

When looking for speakers you need to find one who:

- ▶ speaks on a subject of interest to your guests
- ▶ speaks sufficiently well that your guests will enjoy listening to them
- ▶ will speak for the fee/expenses that you are prepared to pay or who will benefit in some other way by exposure to the attendees.

There are many adequate speakers doing the rounds amongst local business networking groups, or the Professional Speaking Association can advertise to their members that you are looking for a speaker, on a particular topic, for your event.

Promoting your event

In order to promote the event you will need your speaker's subject, summary and profile. You will also need a date and venue.

You may choose to speak yourself in order to demonstrate your expertise. You may prefer a guest speaker with or instead of you.

Eventbrite is a simple online booking system. There is no charge for free tickets but there is a small percentage charge for booking and a second charge if you use them to collect payments. I found the charges worth paying to avoid any hassle and you can also promote your event through Eventbrite itself. I have used other systems as an attendee and found them much harder to book on to events that I wished to attend.

If you are the guest speaker at somebody else's event they should be publicising it, but it is helpful to them and to you to share their publicity and social media posts.

Before the event

Arrive at the venue about an hour beforehand so that you have everything ready for early arrivals.

- ▶ Find the venue's events organiser or your contact.
- ▶ Check that the room is laid out as agreed. We used theatre style for our talks and boardroom style for our workshops. You might also want additional space to circulate for networking.
- ▶ Check that refreshments are available. One venue we used did not turn on the urn so we had no hot water for drinks on arrival.
- ▶ Check that the technology works. Venues will usually provide the projector and you can usually negotiate this and flip charts in the room price.
- ▶ Lay out name badges and signing-in sheets if you are using these.

Speaking for yourself

Speaking for yourself is the best way to promote yourself as an expert rather than relying on your association with a guest speaker. You will need to decide if you are interesting and competent enough to do this.

I was fortunate to go to a school where we learned how to speak publicly so I was prepared to give it a go. In order to focus on the terrifying prospect of speaking I arranged for a professional events organiser and one of our team to take care of everything else on the night.

I chose a non-financial topic in order to be of the broadest interest and to emphasise that we were business advisers and not just accountants. I like to type up my talk longhand and double spaced. I then create PowerPoint slides which are mainly pictures unless words or numbers are necessary.

The aim is to practise my talk sufficiently that I do not need notes or crib cards and definitely do *not* need to read from slides.

There are plenty of books on public speaking, or you can join Toastmasters or the Professional Speaking Association where you can learn from experts.

My personal opinion is that I would rather hear a well-read speech (with a bit of eye contact) than a poor talk that wanders off the topic.

Speaking at someone else's event

This is the easiest way to promote yourself and your business in front of a new audience. You will need to be a reasonable standard to be invited to be a guest speaker. You may also need to be a little cheeky volunteering. It is up to you to negotiate fee, expenses or other benefits.

You may be happy with the exposure or wish to include contact information in delegate packs. We always provided our guest speakers with a video of their talk and contact details of the videographer in case they wanted it edited in any way.

You will need to provide a photograph and a bit about yourself and your talk to include in any advance publicity. Agree with your host how you want to be introduced. It is normal to provide a couple of sentences for them to read out but this may need to be adapted to tie in with the overall event.

Agree with your host about 'selling from the stage'. While this is usually frowned upon it is common to close with a call to action to contact you about X or an invitation to Y as the price for an unpaid talk.

Video and photographs

It is easy to arrange for a professional videographer to record live seminars. The videos of my talks were always edited to 'cup of tea length' for our website, YouTube channel and to share on social media. In the early days it was quite useful for me to watch these back in order to identify areas for improvements. The clips themselves were also useful to share with prospective and existing clients, and the most popular one was on cash flow.

You can also use the opportunity to ask for some video testimonials on the events and on your services in general.

Goody bags and promotional goods

It is always nice to give a parting gift. Promotional gifts are a great way to keep your name in front of people. When first starting up you need to consider minimum order quantities and where you will store the items. This made branded pens our first choice. Nobody ever refuses a pen and, if they get lost, they're still useful advertising. I carried a handful in my bag at all times.

Of course we included some of our printed literature but people will only hang on to this if they're interested in using your services in the near future.

We also used our signature jelly beans (bean growers; not just bean counters) in small wedding favour bags.

Our next promo ventures were shopping list pads and then water bottles. The latter was prompted by my cycling friends and my kids always losing theirs. I figured that either they would hang on to their bottles for a whole term or at least the brand would be out there somewhere.

Branded carrier bags were a great way to get people walking down the street with our name on show, and we soon took to using these to store and return any paper books that we received from clients.

Once we had our own meeting room we stocked up on branded mugs for visitors to use and to be taken away in goody bags. These do take up quite a bit of space and can't easily be carried around or posted out. Give away as much as possible. Promotional goods sitting in the marketing cupboard are not doing anything for you.

Include gifts and material from your guest speakers in order to help pro-mote their business as a thank you. We also had promo items from ICAEW who sponsored a few of our events in the early days.

Repurposing content

This is about making the most of your content. The same content could fairly easily be reused:

- ▶ Live seminar
- ▶ Short videos on YouTube, your website and shared via social media
- ▶ Each talk could be split into about three articles for third parties
- ▶ Each talk could be split into about three blogs which could also be shared on social media

- ▶ Some of the content could be made into help sheets
- ▶ Some of the content forms the basis of this book

Webinars

The advantage of webinars is that they are cheap and easy to run and people can watch them from their own desk or home. We ran a few of these at 8 pm for just 30 minutes. Nobody can see if you're presenting to an audience of one or 100 and, if you record the webinar, you can reuse it again and again. Learn from my mistake and do remember to press the record button! I now write it onto my talk notes.

If you're shy about public speaking you can even read from your script but do try not to sound as though you're doing this. I used to start the webinar with a live camera on me to say hello and then switch to slides that I could talk over.

The downside of webinars is that there is no opportunity for networking or getting to know your audience.

Other events you can run

Bookkeeping/software training

We used to run regular Xero bookkeeping workshops from 6 pm to 8 pm. These were introduced in order to provide basic training and to answer lots of clients queries in one go. We also opened them up to the public for a small fee. Having clients and non-clients in a room together led to our clients providing live testimonials to the non-clients and doing our marketing for us.

In advertising these events we looked more proactive than many competitors and also advertised and demonstrated that we were Xero experts. We received many requests for a couple of hours' individual tuition from non-clients who were self-taught. We used to charge for this time at our offices or the client's, and our head bookkeeper, who carried out all this training, was excellent at selling our accountancy and business advice services as well as demonstrating how friendly and approachable we were. I think that most people who paid for this help came on board for additional services a year or so later.

Strategy days

We used to run strategic planning days and budget days as stand-alone training for clients and non-clients. Both were run from 10 am to 3 pm with a brief sandwich lunch. We had up to six businesses in these workshops so they could share ideas. They were also useful for clients with multiple directors, each with their own agenda as regards income, capital growth, succession planning and so on.

In helping clients to put together their plans we were also able to identify where they needed additional assistance from us or trusted associates.

Pitfalls to avoid

▶ Have competent speakers even if this limits your role to that of host/master of ceremonies

▶ Allow for no-shows when confirming numbers for venues

▶ If speaking yourself then do get plenty of practice and avoid 'death by PowerPoint'

Summary

▶ Decide on your target audience.

▶ Pick a time and date.

▶ Find a suitable venue.

▶ Decide whether to charge attendees and, if so, how much.

▶ Find a speaker and get their marketing blurb well in advance.

▶ Write your own talk and marketing blurb.

▶ Set up your Eventbrite page or other booking website.

▶ Promote the event like mad.

▶ Practise your talk.

▶ Prepare name badges and goody bags.

▶ Arrive at the venue early and check out the tech, booking in and refreshments.

▶ If you are speaking yourself have somebody else to check in guests.

▶ Don't forget a call to action, for example a special offer such as a half-price strategy day.

▶ Follow up afterwards with attendees and non-attendees. We used to send a link to the videos on the website.

Chapter 16

Buying a business

Buying a business is one way to grow your business quickly rather than the slow process of growing organically. It may also be something to consider if you wish to break into a certain field.

Pros of buying

- ▶ Grow your business faster than you would organically
- ▶ Roll out your successful processes to more clients
- ▶ Economies of scale
- ▶ Move into a new area; geographically or technically
- ▶ Buy out a competitor

Cons of buying

- ▶ Cost
- ▶ Time taken to integrate new business and staff
- ▶ Time taken for handover and to reassure new clients
- ▶ May have different ways of working so clients have a different expectation
- ▶ Buying somebody else's problem clients/jobs as they may not have been as diligent as you in improving or moving these along

Finding a business to buy

Accountancy businesses are in short supply. Many sole practitioners either allow their business to run down gradually over time so that they can reduce their workload as they get deeper into retirement, or they are sold to larger companies who just want to acquire the client list.

There are specialist brokers dealing with the buying and selling of accountancy practices and it is usually the buyer who pays their fees. Apart from the cost of a little proactive searching most fees are only payable on successful completion of a sale and they are based on a multiple of the gross recurring income (GRI).

The agent will provide you with a shortlist of businesses to buy, showing:

- ▶ size of the practice
- ▶ client breakdown by unincorporated, limited, personal tax and audit
- ▶ approximate location

- number of staff
- whether premises are available
- whether the business is portable to another office/location.

Once you have signed a non-disclosure agreement (NDA) you will be able to see:

- previous years' accounts and management accounts
- unnamed client lists with fee, work done and age of each client
- unnamed details of staff with position, qualification, hours and so on.

This is the stage at which you would probably meet the vendor.

Why acquisitions don't proceed

When I first set up my business I was constantly on the lookout for a suitable company to buy and I had preliminary talks with a few. These are some of the reasons why an acquisition might not proceed beyond the enquiry stage:

- Mismatch on requirements to retain staff and premises.
- Mismatch in IT systems means additional work to integrate.
- Mismatch in clients means that they are not desirable or they would take additional work to integrate.
- Mismatch in the way the existing owners work with their clients, meaning that they will not adapt to a new owner.
- Business sale may force a member of staff to leave and clients may follow them instead of staying with the new owner.
- Retiring owners are still hands on and the business is not sufficiently profitable to cover the costs of employing somebody to carry out their work and also cover the repayments and interest on finance.
- The age profile of the clients is similar to that of the retiring owners so there is little prospect of long-term retention.
- Mismatch in fees as retiring owners have not increased fees for some time.
- Retiring owners aren't really ready to retire and hand over.
- Retiring owners overvalue their business for any reason.

Some of these issues can be overcome by adjusting the purchase price but, for others, it is best to walk away.

I did find one practice which was beautifully prepared for sale by the part-time owner but I eventually, and reluctantly, concluded that it was slightly too far away to fit with either my current marketing strategy or my family commitments. This one was really difficult to turn down and I kept having to come back to my little notebook with my primary business purpose.

How much should you pay?

Goodwill

The price for this is a multiplier of GRI. The market rate is between 0.8 and 1.2 times GRI, that is, regular annual fees excluding any one-off work. Things that will affect this multiplier:

- ▶ How good a fit the business is for you
- ▶ If the business will run independently of the retiring owner due to the systems in place and well trained staff
- ▶ The nature of the clients including their age profile. If the clients are all at an age where they are likely to be retiring themselves then they are of less value as you are interested in acquiring future business

Net assets

The value of the net assets that you will acquire is based approximately on their balance sheet values.

Other contract factors

- ▶ Payment period. It is normal for acquisitions to be paid for over a period of one or two years although I have heard of much longer. If your buyer wants payment up front you may discount the price. Depending on the size of the transaction it would be normal to pay your vendor in instalments. This would commonly be half or a third on completion and then two further payments at the 12- and 24-month marks. Some sales involve more frequent payments or a longer payment period. I did hear of a colleague paying over four years.
- ▶ Clawback. If clients do not stay with you then there is usually a provision to clawback the payment on these fees. Clawback can be on individual fees or on total fees including annual price rises. This gives a financial incentive to the seller to ensure a smooth hando-ver. It may be that the vendor wants to be certain of their financial position and will accept a lower fixed price so that the risk of clients leaving is with you, the purchaser.

- ▶ Clawback period. The clawback may be 100 per cent of the lost GRI in the first 12 months and there may be a further 50 per cent clawback for 12–24 months. This reflects the seller's diminishing responsibility for keeping the practice intact.

- ▶ Fees. Some contracts include a clause that fees are not to be increased during the clawback period for fear of clients being priced out of the new business by unscrupulous buyers. It puts an unnecessary pressure on buyers who need to cover inflationary cost increases over the period. It would be more reasonable to agree to charge fees on the same basis or even to agree an annual percentage increase.

- ▶ Non-compete. There will be a period during which the seller cannot act against the interests of the business by offering an alternative accountancy service to their former clients either directly or while working for somebody else. This must be a reasonable restriction overall but it is helpful to find out what your seller intends to do afterwards to ensure that there is no conflict between their old and new work. They should not be allowed to approach existing clients or staff for a period either, although this is always hard to enforce where friendships are involved.

My story

I did buy a bookkeeping practice from a friend who was moving into employment and needed a quick sale and handover to ensure that her clients were looked after. While it is always risky doing business with friends we did ensure that the main details were covered by a written contract. Although I had not been actively looking for a business acquisition it suited me to take on a bookkeeping firm and to introduce the efficiencies of Xero and Receipt Bank, along with the opportunity to add on year-end and management accounting work.

You may have to give a commitment on not increasing fees for 12 months. This is what I did with my acquisition and wish that I had not. When I came to sell my own practice my clients were used to an annual increase so my buyer was only constrained to charging on the same basis, not the same amount. This meant that he could increase fees during the first year in the same way that I would have.

Other considerations

As part of the due diligence process you need to check:

- ▶ the accounts and the assets that you are buying

- ▶ that there are engagement letters and other contracts are in place
- ▶ a sample of working papers and so on
- ▶ the contract itself.

On the day of the sale you should receive:

- ▶ keys
- ▶ passwords
- ▶ engagement letters
- ▶ supplier contracts
- ▶ staff contracts
- ▶ anything else that you need to run the business.

Legals

I would recommend using a solicitor in the process. They will ensure that there are guarantees in the contract if you make discoveries post-sale that did not come to light as part of your due diligence checks. You will also want to put in place some sort of non-compete clause restricting your vendor from competing against you directly or via a third party within a certain geographical radius and within a certain period of time. There are other restrictions that you may wish to put in place concerning poaching both clients and staff.

Insurance

You need to ensure that insurance is in place from day one and, as soon as possible, reissue engagement letters and 64-8s in the name of the new firm. If you are buying the shares of the company then you have longer to arrange to transfer bank accounts. As an attempt to smooth the handover I was appointed director prior to the final sale. We tried to set me up as a bank signatory beforehand too but your vendor might prefer to wait until after the sale. Any leases and so on may need to be transferred into the buyer's name.

Share or asset purchase

This process is all much simpler if you are buying the shares in the company; however, you will also be taking on all the assets and liabilities of the business too. A share sale is simpler as the bank accounts and office lease will be in the company name. This allows you to transfer everything at your convenience. The alternative is to arrange to transfer all contracts and insurances on the day of sale.

You and the vendor will also want to consider the tax aspects of each type of transfer in your particular circumstances.

Meeting the team

The other thing that you will probably want to do early on is to speak to the staff. The business that I bought had three subcontractors. My preference was to employ my team and so, when telling them about the acquisition, I offered them all employed positions. One took me up on this offer and the other two preferred to remain as subcontractors. We arranged a dinner in a local pub so that both teams could meet and get to know each other.

Of the two subcontractors one remained with us for just over a year until she had grown her own bookkeeping practice and we parted on good terms; she took one small client by agreement. The other told all the clients she worked with that we were not keeping her on so they had to choose between her and the new company. I can't blame the clients for choosing the person they knew. There seemed little point in telling them that she had lied as I would clearly not be retaining such a dishonest subcontractor. It is one of the few times that people have let me down, and the vendor was absolutely distraught at the betrayal both personally and because it would reduce the value of the business she was selling to me.

Taking on more staff meant that we were bursting at the seams in our existing office (even with storing most of the marketing materials, stationery and archiving off site) so I had to find larger premises in a hurry. Do build this into your expansion plans.

Handover

As part of the acquisition you should expect a period of about two months post-sale for the seller to make all necessary introductions and to generally smooth the way. Any work after this handover period may be in the seller's interest to minimise client loss and clawback, but it would be normal to pay a consultancy rate for any material work.

It is important that you take the time to find a company which is a good fit for your business as this will help clients to settle into the new regime more easily and they are more likely to stay with you. You and the seller will need to identify key clients to visit or at least telephone to make personal introductions. These visits are often made before the sale takes place.

For the remaining 'new' clients and any introducers and suppliers, you will need to agree a letter with the vendor. The emphasis should be on business as usual but, if there are to be changes in staff or location, this should be made clear and the benefits explained to the clients. You may wish to let your existing clients know what is happening too.

Publicity

Buying a business provides a good opportunity to raise your profile with a press release.

Avoiding pitfalls

With the benefit of hindsight I would prefer to grow organically rather than by acquisition because:

▶ in integrating new clients and systems I was unable to focus on growing the business organically

▶ with so many new clients coming on board at once I was quite exhausted trying to manage it all as quickly as possible

▶ in buying another business you are inheriting different problems and client expectations that you would normally filter at the initial meeting stage.

If you are not confident in your ability to grow organically, then you should certainly consider growth by acquisition.

Summary

Things to consider when buying a business are:

▶ Finding a good fit.
▶ Agreeing the price.
▶ Agreeing payment terms.
▶ Share acquisition or net assets.
▶ Meeting the team.
▶ Client handover.

Chapter 17
Buying a franchise

Why buy a franchise?

Building a business from scratch is not for everybody, especially if you have limited business experience. Buying an existing business can short-cut this business experience but can be expensive.

Buying a franchise allows you to buy a framework for running your business and also a brand and some marketing.

Advantages of a franchise

- ▶ Established brand name
- ▶ Procedures manual for your business
- ▶ Training
- ▶ Software
- ▶ Access to specialists
- ▶ Lead generation
- ▶ Marketing material or marketing done for you
- ▶ A peer group of other franchisees

Disadvantages of a franchise

- ▶ Cost of all of the above both up front and ongoing
- ▶ Restrictions on what you can do (in order to align with the brand)

Two options

Cheapaccounting.co.uk and TaxAssist Accountants are two common but very different franchises and their main offering are summarised in Table 2.

Table 2: Cheapaccounting.co.uk's and TaxAssist Accountants' main offerings

	Cheapaccounting.co.uk	TaxAssist Accountants
Qualifications required	MAAT, ACCA, ACA, CA, ACAI, ACMA, CIOT or ATT plus acceptance by Cheapaccounting.co.uk network	Accountants and commercially experienced individuals may join TaxAssist Accountants subject to acceptance by the TaxAssist directors
Initial training	Business planning, marketing plan, technical skills assessment, set up of back office and operational processes, and referrals handling. As the franchise consists of qualified accountants no technical training is given on tax and accounts preparation.	An intensive six-week initial training course is provided, followed by a six-month nurture programme. Training covers how to run and grow a practice, bookkeeping, tax, accounts preparation, IT, software, HR, recruitment, marketing and social media.
Suitable for part-time practitioners, e.g. parents, carers and pre-retirees	Low initial investment. The only restriction is that you can't run it just in the evenings or at weekends. Any current contract of employment must allow you to run your own practice alongside your job.	Higher initial investment. The TaxAssist Accountants franchise is a full-time business opportunity, with franchisees supported to run and grow substantial practices. Many operate from multiple premises, with the aim of having a light touch on the business, with staff fully trained and supported by the TaxAssist Accountants Support Centre. This also allows for the possibility of succession planning.
Operational standards	Minimal formalities plus standards and ethics of your professional accountancy body.	Manuals and training provided but some autonomy.
Recognised brand name	Reputable and increasing exposure through expert media appearances and substantial social media presence.	Common due to requirement for shopfront and similar premises alongside TV advertising campaigns and substantial Internet presence.

	Cheapaccounting.co.uk	TaxAssist Accountants
Help provided	Initial training. Mentoring and coaching. Annual conference. Referrals/hot leads. Technical support.	Getting started manual. Initial training. Ongoing training. Online support site. IT and software. Premises support (help finding the right office/ shop and location). Lead generation. National marketing. Technical team. Access to technical specialists. National purchasing deals. Director and franchise development manager visits. Exit planning assistance.
Guarantee to franchisees	12 months subject to terms and conditions (T&Cs). Will refund fee in exchange for your client list.	There can be no guarantee of success, although TaxAssist Accountants has won awards for the level of support on offer to franchisees

Other franchises are available and, if you are thinking seriously of following this route, you should look around for the one which suits you best.

Whichever franchise you choose it is still up to you to make it work. Although buying a franchise will shortcut some of the admin and marketing burden of a new business, your prosperity will still depend on how much work you put in yourself.

Who can help?

If you have read this book and are still feeling overwhelmed then it may be worth your while considering investing in a franchise. For further information see the contacts for Cheapaccounting.co.uk and TaxAssist Accountants.

Summary

▶ Consider a franchise if you are not sure of the business aspects or if you want to shortcut some of the start-up learning.

▶ Different franchises will offer different support so find one which suits your requirements and budget.

▶ A franchise is cheaper than buying an existing business and does not come with any legacy problems as, in theory, you will set up your business properly from the beginning.

▶ You will still need to grow your own business but you will have a lot of support to help you do this.

Chapter 18
Deciding your exit strategy

I keep a Dreams and Desires file, an idea that I got from work that my father was doing with ex-drug addicts in Wiltshire. I think that it is very important to find out what success looks like for different clients. Then we can set about helping them to achieve it through income from their business when trading but also on retirement. It is also useful for us to know what success means to us as it is usually more than just money.

I love hearing how businesses started up in someone's garden shed or on the corner of their kitchen table. It is great to hear how entrepreneurs have taught themselves new skills as their business develops. I love helping those businesses to grow once the owners are in a position to bring in an expert from outside. I particularly like working with accountants.

So this chapter on deciding your exit strategy is about how you eventually retire from your business.

Issues to consider

There are several ways of generating a retirement fund from your business when the time comes. The best way for you will depend on the nature of your business and whether you wish to retire completely or just scale things back a little.

Some options are:

- ▶ Pay into a standard pension fund
- ▶ Pay into a SIPP
- ▶ Take cash out of your business to invest in property – residential or commercial
- ▶ Sell all or part of your business to a third party or to a management buyout (MBO)
- ▶ Franchise your business
- ▶ Put a manager into your business and step back

Pension funds

Let's deal with the conventional one first. Pension funds are a tax-efficient savings plan. You get tax relief on payments into the plan but you pay tax when you take it out in retirement, although usually at a lower rate because you are not earning so much. When you retire there are a variety of things that you can do with these funds to generate an income throughout your retirement.

Your pension is a tax-efficient way to pay yourself if you don't need the money today. It is also useful for pushing you back under certain thresholds so that you stay within a lower tax band or get to keep your child benefit.

If you are considering a pension fund then you should speak to a qualified IFA on the best approach for your particular circumstances. They can also advise on SIPPs.

Property investment

You will pay tax on the cash you take out of the business to purchase all or part of your property.

A lot of people like to invest their spare cash in buy-to-let properties for income and capital gain. Remember that the increase in price of your additional property is taxable. HMRC are now checking the land registers to spot sales of properties that are not your principal primary residence (aka home).

With increases in stamp duty and the relief lost on mortgage interest, property is not a tax-efficient investment so you will need to make bigger gains through net rental income or capital gains on eventual sale.

Commercial property

Commercial property investments can be put into a SIPP and can be more tax effective. If you own your own business premises then this is something that you could look into.

Franchising your business

This is best done with the help of a specialist to help you with standard systems, registering intellectual property, marketing to end users, marketing to franchisees, etc.

Sale of your business

You can sell your business to a third party or an MBO.

You can sell all or part of your business.

If you sell all of your business you may be able or even required to continue working at some level for a little while longer.

If you sell part of your business this will generate a lump sum that you can invest in any of the other schemes or spend it all on sweets.

Remember that in having a partner you will no longer have complete control of your company. A new owner or majority shareholder may take your business, which you have carefully built up, and do things that you do not agree with. Will they look after your customers? Your staff? Will you care? If you are selling a large proportion then you must be prepared for this. If you are selling just part of your business then don't forget to get a good shareholder agreement.

How to value your business

Ultimately your business is worth what somebody is prepared to pay for it. Accountancy practices are fairly saleable and there are a number of specialist brokers. You can expect 0.8–1.2 times GRI.

There is usually a clawback arrangement of some sort to take account of clients who move on because they do not feel tied to the business without you there or for any other reason.

You can arrange to sell the net assets of the business plus the goodwill/ client list or you can sell the shares in your company. Your buyer may have a preference.

A buyer may be interested in your premises or they may wish to relocate your business.

You must also consider any staff. Will they transfer with the business or will you need to make them redundant?

Things that will increase the multiplier and hence the overall value of your business are systems. The better the business can run without you personally the more valuable it will still be when you step out of the picture. Many of the things that you would do to franchise also apply here. If your business will run smoothly without you at the helm then it is a true business and not self-employment.

If you are even thinking of selling your business then you should start preparing three to five years before sale. It may well be worth inviting a business adviser to come and give you the sort of independent review that you cannot carry out yourself.

You may even need a different structure for your business. The classic example is that accountancy practices and other professional service companies are sold based mainly on a factor of turnover, whereas they will probably have been run on a day-to-day basis to maximise your profit.

As a majority shareholder working in the business you will probably qualify for Entrepreneurs Relief but do consider the tax position for silent partners.

You need to agree when you will be paid. All at once or over a couple of years?

Who accepts liability for previous debts or for rectifying poor work or faulty goods? You will need to provide up to six years' run-off insurance to cover any professional indemnity claims relating to work carried out under your supervision. This should cover all professional claims and protect you from personal liability.

How to increase the value of your business

- ▶ Systemise to make it less dependent on you and key staff in the event that they also leave
- ▶ Systemise to maintain high quality/service levels
- ▶ Make it less location dependent or move premises if these are not for sale
- ▶ Increase profitability or turnover
- ▶ Put procedures in an operating manual

Management buyout

This is similar to a third-party sale except that you will have a good team to ensure that your clients and staff are looked after. This is a much simpler process but you may receive a lower price or payment over a longer period.

Working part-time

You can scale back your business and deal with fewer clients. This will provide you with lower income but with more time. Your overheads may be disproportionately high. As with a start-up you will still need to pay for a full practising certificate, software licences and so on whether you use them full-time or part-time.

You may be able to sell part of your business or gradually run it down.

Employ a manager

With the right person to take care of the day-to-day running of the company you can dip in and out at your leisure. This will be easier if your business is heavily systemised. There's that word again!

You could outsource more and spend a proportion of your profits to buy yourself more time.

There are so many possible solutions and all of them will require some sort of preparation to get you the best deal. It is worth having at least some idea a long way beforehand of which way you hope to go so that you can structure your business or your pension plan or your property portfolio in plenty of time.

Summary

▶ Decide if you will fund your retirement out of the business income or whether your business can be sold to generate a lump sum.

▶ Systemising your business is a worthwhile exercise in most cases. As well as increasing efficiency while you are running the business, it will make it easier to run part-time, to franchise or to increase the value on sale.

▶ Documenting your systems will also help with most of these actions.

▶ Plan early so that you have time to save into a pension, extract cash in a tax-effective manner for investment elsewhere or to prepare the business for sale.

Chapter 19
Monitoring your management
accounts and KPIs

Running a business requires more than just statutory accounts once a year.

What you need in your toolbox

- ▶ Strategic plan
- ▶ Forecasts and budgets
- ▶ Actual monthly performance of all your KPIs
- ▶ Annual accounts
- ▶ Comparison with previous years
- ▶ Comparison with others in your industry
- ▶ List of gross recurring fees for business valuation
- ▶ Improvement plans
- ▶ Ideas – plenty of them

Initially my business plan was little more than a few ideas and some estimated numbers, but in 2012, after getting fit and running the Bristol 10 km, I wrote what I called my Icarus Budget. As the name might suggest it was a huge aspiration and I blame the endorphin high. This is the five-year plan which turned my one-man band into a proper cloud accounting business. I've since made a point of writing my plans when I'm feeling at my most positive and then reviewing the actions at a later date. The masterplan is broken down into the actions needed to achieve the results and the key figures to check that I am carrying out those actions. I still believe that the most useful KPIs are those which monitor actions rather than results. You should still monitor the results of KPIs, of course, to ensure that they are the right actions.

Typical KPIs you might choose to measure in your accountancy business

Marketing

- ▶ Speaking events. Speaking at more events will increase your profile and allow you to demonstrate your expertise.
- ▶ Articles/blogs. These are another way of demonstrating your expertise and may be a better format for many. Do try to avoid dry technical subjects which risk sending your readers to sleep. You are selling yourself to non-accountants who expect you to know this stuff so that they don't need to.

- Social media posts. A great way of increasing your profile and networking with a wider range of people (see Chapter 11, 'Networking through social media').

- Klout score. This is an indication of your social media reach, and the extent that people are interacting with you and the content that you are posting. Take this figure with a pinch of salt; it is easy to increase your Klout score by posting pictures of cute puppies but this may not convert into enquiries.

- Number of enquiries and their source. This is to try to understand which of your marketing activities is most effective.

- Number of networking events. This increases your profile. One-to-one coffees are often much more productive than some of the larger events as you can make a quality connection rather than just collect business cards.

Clients

- Number of clients (with signed engagement letters). It is useful to track this as much of your admin cost is per client, no matter whether they are large or small.

- GRI. That is, usual fees expected to recur next year so excluding one-offs.

- Average fee. The higher this is the better as this reflects the increased quality of clients.

Efficiency

- Number of clients on Xero or your chosen system. You can operate much more efficiently if all your clients operate the same software in which you are an expert. I'm not suggesting that you force clients on to unsuitable software for your convenience. They should be on the most appropriate financial software even if this means moving to another accountant.

- Number of jobs outstanding. That is, past their year end but not yet received in the office.

- Number of jobs received but not completed. Once the client has sent their books to you or given you access to their completed bookkeeping system the clock is ticking.

- Turnaround time. We defined this as the time from receipt in the office to sending out final accounts (we rarely bothered with drafts as queries could be answered with a phone call or email). This was an important timescale for some clients, whereas others weren't bothered. Our aim was for six weeks to allow us time to schedule the work and deal with any queries.

Financial

▶ Work in progress (WIP)/debtors (also known as lockup). Your cash is tied up in uninvoiced work and unpaid bills. If you read Chapter 13, 'Controlling your cash flow', you will see that, with fixed fees paid in advance, it is possible to have 'negative work in progress'.

▶ Profit and cash in bank, although these figures are the result of getting the other indicators right.

Planning and forecasting

You need to know which direction you want your business to take in order to decide the actions to get you there. This requires some sort of a plan.

A detailed 12-month plan combined with a five-year plan is a good way to set this out. This should provide you with an action plan and also a marketing plan to generate the enquiries to grow your business.

Each month you need to sit down and compare your KPIs and financials to your plan to ensure that you are on track. If there are any shortfalls you need to understand what has happened and put together a plan to get back on track.

Spend time on the handful of KPIs which affect your business most. While we were relatively cash rich, cash flow forecasting was not critical so I didn't spend time on this.

Summary

▶ Work out where you want your business to be and by when then decide what KPIs will drive your business forwards.

▶ Measure these KPIs on at least a weekly basis; I had mine on a whiteboard in my office for all the team to see.

▶ Change your three to six main KPIs as you focus on improving different aspects of your business.

▶ Consider having a board, a business coach or similar for account-ability as well as guidance.

▶ Celebrate your successes with your team.

Chapter 20
Helping the wider community

Chapter 20   Helping the wider community

We have always believed in contributing to the local community but have also found it a very good way to promote the business and to provide a lot of job satisfaction.

Pros of community work

- Increased profile in the community, some of which is with other local businesses
- Creating referrers and ambassadors for the brand
- Identifying potential employees
- Helping others
- Improving the community in which you live/work
- Opportunities for PR articles
- Doing something you enjoy for the benefit of the business

Cons of community work

- Cost compared to uncertain returns
- Scattergun approach to marketing as much of it affects non-businesses
- Time spent in carrying out activities is non-fee earning

Issues to consider

There are a number of ways to contribute to the local community and some will be more appealing than others. As an owner-managed business you may decide that personal satisfaction offsets some of the time/cost involved. For instance, my love of sports meant that I was happy to sponsor local grass-roots and charity football matches with a low chance of commercial reward. I was fortunate that most of these did reap financial benefits.

There are several ways that you might choose to 'pay it forward'.

Commercial karma

Helping others through referrals and introductions costs you nothing but, if you introduce the right people, it generates a great deal of goodwill from both parties to the introduction. For this reason you might want to be careful who you introduce. Sometimes I make qualified introductions along the lines of 'I haven't done business with them but they are good people so please let me know how you get on.'

Some of the closed networking groups encourage such referrals but focus more on quantity than quality. If you are a member of such a group you should get to know your fellow members and exactly how they can (or can't) help your contacts. A poor referral wastes everybody's time and reflects badly on you. In this type of group you should also be clear what makes a good referral for you. When we stopped doing tax for individuals and introduced a minimum fee we still received enquiries from referrers who didn't know this.

Do not expect reciprocal referrals; this is primarily about helping others but it will generate goodwill in the business community as a whole.

Helping schools

When helping schools you are in a position to both mould what they do in order to generate more useful employees in the future and also to talent spot individuals whom you might wish to employ yourself. As a parent I'm keen to think that others, in turn, will do this for my children.

The things that we have done include:

- ▶ Mock interviews. They usually follow a pattern prescribed by the school.
- ▶ Work experience. You will need to have a risk assessment for young people and employee liability insurance but your local council will help with the formalities. We provided a mixture of work projects requiring a little learning and then minimal supervision. We also took our students along to a couple of networking events and client meetings. Do get permission from the event organiser and your client beforehand! We arranged for all students to sign our confidentiality contract. While not enforceable in law it served as a reminder to them of the importance of confidentiality in our profession. Work experience can also act as an extended interview and we found an apprentice in this way.
- ▶ Careers fairs. We prepared for these in the same way as for business/trade fairs. There is no charge to exhibit and you have the opportunity to talk to lots of potential recruits about accountancy or starting a business in general. Most are accompanied by parents who may be business owners themselves so it helps to increase your profile in the wider community. We provided goody bags with our name on that we hoped reminded others of us for a while longer.

Charity pro bono and how to say no

A quick online search shows that there are over 35 charities and community groups in our village. All of these require a treasurer and some need an independent review.

There may be particular charities that appeal to your heart or your interests so prioritise these. Spending five hours counting cash after a school Parent-Teacher Association (PTA) event may not feel like the best use of your time and expertise but it provides a clear role model for your own children.

In addition I set aside a budget for pro bono work. The idea was that we would charge commercial fees for the work (we are not a charity after all, and still need to pay staff and bills) but would subsidise part or all of the fee from the pro bono budget. When the budget was gone we would explain this and also that, as the budget was a percentage of our fees, we could give more as the business grew. This made it easy to say 'no' while also pointing out the link that we could give more if we received more.

Sponsorship

I love sport, especially grass-roots sport, so I loved contributing to local football and rugby clubs and a few charity events. The commercial benefits from each club/event included our name on advertising boards, shirts, programmes, websites and so on. The clubs also provided opportunities for PR in local publications and some arranged networking events or lunches for sponsors.

I found this a great way of combining business and pleasure so I was always nicely surprised when we picked up new clients as a result. It was definitely an opportunity to meet people with similar interests, which led to these new clients, so do go along and be seen at the club/event so that you are more than just an anonymous advert.

By sponsoring events or groups that you enjoy it will feel like so much more than just an overhead. Business should be enjoyable whenever possible.

Always check what benefits you will receive in exchange for your sponsorship and make sure that these match with your personal requirements too. Some sports sponsorship provides an opportunity to meet your favourite players.

Do you have useful facilities?

Small businesses and networking groups need meeting space. If you have unused training or meeting rooms you can allow clients and other business groups to use these for their own meetings.

One training client regularly brought growing businesses into our premises for their events and the only cost to us was tea, coffee and biscuits. This was exactly our target market and we didn't have to do anything more than put the kettle on.

We also hosted events for the local Chamber of Commerce. These were events which I would have attended anyway but they allowed us to increase our profile in the local business community. We only had to provide basic refreshments or a few additional items at cost.

Do you get discounts when purchasing items which you can allow community groups to share if they need to purchase similar items?

Collaboration

For a couple of years I belonged to a formal collaboration group of non-local accountants. As we were not in direct competition we helped each other out with ideas and what had or hadn't worked for us. I received lots of help from others in the group when introducing services or software that they had already tried and I hope that they gained as much from me. I still keep in touch with them along with others in an informal network.

I'm always keen to have coffee with other local accountants to see where we can help each other and also, exactly, where we are in competition. As we were too small to be all things to all men I believe in referring enquiries to the best accountant for the client and this wasn't always us. We didn't do tax for individuals and we were not cost-effective for the smallest, lifestyle businesses. At the other end of the scale we did not always have the specialist knowledge that certain businesses needed so it was right to refer them to others whom we knew and trusted.

Ethics

While we all sign up to the ethics of our relevant bodies, there are broader decisions to make in how we operate our businesses.

My elderly marketing lecturer at university summed it up when he told all us keen youngsters that business ethics are often subjective so we should decide for ourselves what we considered right and wrong and then stick to it. We may all differ on exactly where we draw the line on certain issues. I assume that you would never support tax evasion but how do you stand on advanced tax planning? On salary versus dividends? How much work a spouse should do to justify a salary? Be very clear on what you will and won't do and never change this because you are desperate to keep a client.

Avoiding pitfalls

▶ Decide in advance how much time/money you are prepared to pay for things with little direct commercial benefit but other rewards such as showing corporate social responsibility (CSR) or just being a responsible business.

▶ Do not be sucked into taking on too much pro bono work in the hope that it will lead to something more; it usually doesn't.

▶ Remember that some charities can afford to pay for your services so save your pro bono work for others which can't.

▶ It is ok to say 'no'.

▶ Always invoice your charities even if you show a 100 per cent discount so that they appreciate the value of your services.

Summary

▶ Work out the benefits you will definitely receive for your time/cash.

▶ Work out the benefits you will possibly receive for your time/cash.

▶ Some of these benefits may not be purely commercial.

▶ Assess your ROI on each activity.

▶ Some charities/community causes may be more appealing to you than others; you are free to choose.

▶ You can, and should, say 'no' to things which do not satisfy you financially or that do not fit with your values as the business owner.

Conclusion

Running a business is hard and it is not for everyone.

As the owner the buck stops with you so surround yourself with a supportive network in your business life and home life.

Systemise your business as much as possible to make your own life easier, to allow you to expand and to eventually sell the business.

Never undervalue yourself. A good accountant can really add value to their clients; even the smallest ones will benefit from peace of mind. Charge enough to provide the agreed service level.

The next steps that you might take as a result of reading this book:

- ▶ Set up and grow your business using this book and other resources such as a business coach or adviser
- ▶ Look into buying a ready-made business and use a few tips from this book to grow it
- ▶ Look into buying a franchise and use a few tips from this book to grow it
- ▶ Realise that running your own business is not right for you at the moment

Whatever you decide, enjoy the ride and do let me know how you're getting on or if you have any good news to share: numbersbusiness@hudsonbusiness.co.uk.

Further resources

Chapter 2, 'Establishing your systems and services'

- Ashford, James (2016) *Selling to Serve: The breakthrough sales system for cloud accountants*. CreateSpace Independent Publishing Platform.
- Gerber, Michael E. (2001) *The E-Myth Revisited: Why most small businesses don't work and what to do about it*. HarperBusiness.

Chapter 3, 'Dealing with the formalities'

- FSB for employment law, tax advice and assorted legal contract: www.fsb.org.uk

Chapter 7, 'Building your team'

- DNT Chartered Accountants for outsourcing to Northern Ireland: www.dntca.com
- SMART Support for Business – outsourced appraisals and DISC profiling: www.smartsupportforbusiness.co.uk
- 2020 Innovation for continuing professional development training: www.the2020group.com
- www.xero.com for Xero certification and training

Chapter 8, 'Choosing your software'

- Capitalise: www.capitalise.com
- Chaser.io: www.chaser.io
- Freeagent: www.freeagent.com
- Futrli: www.futrli.com
- GoProposal™: www.goproposal.com
- Hosted Accountants: www.hostedaccountants.co.uk
- Logical Office: www.logical-office.com
- Moneysoft Payroll Manager: www.moneysoft.co.uk
- Practice Ignition: www.practiceignition.com
- QBO: https://quickbooks.intuit.com/uk/
- Receipt Bank: www.receipt-bank.com
- Sage: www.sage.com

- ▶ Signable: www.signable.co.uk
- ▶ Spider Group (hosting): www.spidergroup.com
- ▶ Spotlight: www.spotlightreporting.com
- ▶ Taxcalc: www.taxcalc.com
- ▶ Tripcatcher: www.tripcatcherapp.com
- ▶ VT Software: www.vtsoftware.co.uk
- ▶ Xero: www.xero.com/uk

Chapter 9, 'Marketing your business'

- ▶ Thomas, Bryony (2013) *Watertight Marketing: Delivering long-term sales results*. Ecademy Press Ltd.
- ▶ 2020 Innovation for content: www.the2020group.com
- ▶ Valuable content: www.valuablecontent.co.uk
- ▶ Watertight Marketing™ training and consulting: www.watertightmarketing.com

Chapter 11, 'Networking through social media'

- ▶ Digital Mums: www.digitalmums.com
- ▶ Hootsuite: www.hootsuite.com

Chapter 12, 'Moving into premises'

- ▶ Claiming use of home: https://www.gov.uk/expenses-if-youre-self-employed
- ▶ Principle Private Residence Relief: https://www.gov.uk/tax-sell-home

Chapter 15, 'Speaking at and organising events'

- ▶ Professional Speaking Association: www.thepsa.co.uk
- ▶ Eventbrite: www.eventbrite.co.uk

Chapter 18, 'Deciding your exit strategy'

- ▶ Sale of business assets versus shares: http://ukbusinessbrokers.com/asset-sale-vs-share-sale-whats-better-deal/
- ▶ Entrepreneurs Relief: https://www.gov.uk/entrepreneurs-relief

About the author

Della Hudson has been working in accountancy since 1989 when she first started training as a chartered accountant after completing her degree in chemistry and management at City, University of London. Apart from a brief spell in IT she spent most of her career working in industry and helping to run UK subsidiaries of large multinationals.

In 2009, with two small children, Della set up her own chartered accountancy practice, Hudson Business Accountants and Advisers, on her kitchen table and grew it to a team of eight people in independent offices before selling up in 2018.

With no thoughts of retiring Della now works as a speaker (Accountex), writer (Accountingweb) and consultant to accountants and other businesses alongside her non-executive director and finance director roles.

In her free time Della enjoys the swim, bike, run of triathlons and cooking and eating with friends.